Yellowstone Vegetation

5/27/92

Yellowstone Vegetation

Consequences of Environment and History in a Natural Setting

Don G. Despain
Research Biologist
Yellowstone National Park

ROBERTS RINEHART PUBLISHERS
Boulder   Santa Barbara   West Cork

International Standard Book Number 0-911797-75-0
Library of Congress Catalog Card Number 90-61588
Printed in the United States of America
Designed by Linda Seals

Publication of this book was made possible, in part,
by a grant from the Loyal Order of the Moose, coordinated
through the Fire Recovery Fund, National Park Foundation

Contents

List of Figures

List of Tables

Preface

Plants or plant products surround us. They supply us with food and protect our bodies from heat, cold, and disease organisms. They decorate our surroundings and delight our souls. Even the air we breathe has been cleansed of harmful gases and infused with life-giving oxygen by plants. Yet, for most of us, botanical knowledge is limited to the names of some house plants and a few plants in our yards and gardens.

Most people know little about the adaptations plants have made to survive, about the large number of interactions between individuals of the same and different species, or about the physical and chemical defenses plants have developed against insects and grazing animals. The results of plants' struggles for survival are exhibited by those species growing together in plant communities distributed across the landscape. The study of this distribution and the reasons for it is the domain of vegetation scientists.

All species of life, plant or animal, have at least some effect on their environment as a consequence of life processes. Species that become too disruptive may destroy the very ecosystems upon which they depend. The human species has developed the capacity to be a part of most environments capable of supporting life; human demands and their by-products affect virtually every ecosystem on the earth. Our capability to destroy these ecosystems gives us the responsibility for their preservation, and our existence on this planet depends on how well we succeed in this responsibility. To succeed, we must understand ecosystem processes and parts.

Yellowstone National Park provides opportunities for close study of a naturally operating ecosystem. It is a place where we may see the workings of an ecosystem that is as free as possible from human interference or manipulation. In the more than 25 years that I have intensively studied plants and the 18 years that I have studied the vegetation of Yellowstone National Park, I have grown to appreciate this part of the natural world with a reverence that is difficult to explain. In the following pages, I will share some of the things I have learned about the plant life of Yellowstone. I will describe much of the environment of Yellowstone National Park and discuss most of the plant communities that result from the plant-environment interactions. I hope to help readers better understand and, perhaps, better appreciate the plant life of Yellowstone National Park.

Acknowledgments

Many people helped bring about this book. Parents, colleagues, teachers, instructors, advisors, and supervisors kindled in me the spark and kept alive the fires of curiosity about the vegetative world around me. Though you are unnamed here, know that I will be forever grateful that you opened my eyes to this complex and beautiful world.

Many secretaries spent hours proofreading and typing, but I want to thank especially Margaret Holland, not only for her efforts over the years but also for her faith in me. Several people read various drafts of this manuscript and made suggestions for improvement; I thank especially Susan Mills, Paul Schullery, Doug Houston, Dennis Knight, and Bill Romme. The book is much better as a result of their efforts. Dave Mattson was kind enough to provide the drawings of the cover-type silhouettes.

Introduction

Much of the beauty of Yellowstone National Park is provided by the plant cover draped across its mountains and valleys. Standing on a high point in the park, such as Mount Washburn, one can see below a rich tapestry of colors. Most pieces of the mosaic are subtle shades of green that differ very little from their neighbors. Close observation, however, reveals darker, bluish green Douglas-fir stands; dark green spruce-fir stands; and yellowish green young lodgepole pine stands. These stands form sharp contrasts against the browns and blacks of recently burned forests, the rich green of meadows, or the gray of alpine ridges.

These different plant communities provide homes and food for a wide variety of animals ranging from the magnificent grizzly bear to minute insects, and an animal's presence is often a direct result of the plant species growing in an area. The ability of plants to capture sunlight and convert it to chemical energy supports the large herds of elk, bison, deer, and mountain sheep that attract our attention. With the exception of the thermal features of the park, vegetation is intertwined with most of the magic that is Yellowstone.

Yellowstone's location greatly influences the type of vegetation that can grow there. The park is between the 44th and 45th parallels, halfway between the equator and the north pole. Air warmed and made light by the intense tropical sun wends northward to be replaced by the heavier, cooler air of the far north. These air movements are turned westward by the rotation of the earth and, according to fluid dynamics, move and twist in interesting ways to produce a temperate climate for the park.

Located between the 110th and 111th west longitudes,

Yellowstone is well into the interior of the North American continent, straddling the Continental Divide. Mountains on its west boundary drop onto the intermountain plains while those of the east boundary drop onto the Great Plains of the Midwest. Elevations within the park vary from 5,265 feet in the north, where the Yellowstone River diverges from the park boundary and flows north into Montana, to several peaks between 10,000 and 11,000 feet along the eastern and northern boundaries. Upper timberline is near 10,000 feet. Most of the park is between 7,000 and 9,000 feet, in the subalpine zone.

The climate is characterized by long, cold winters and short, cool summers. Mean monthly temperature at Lake Yellowstone ranges from 10.7°F to 55.2°F and averages 32.8°F. The extremes recorded to date are –66°F at West Yellowstone in 1933 and 103°F at Gardiner in 1960. Climate will be discussed in greater detail in Part Two.

Total annual precipitation is greatest (about 70 inches) in the southwest corner of the park, where air crossing the Snake River plain first meets a topographic rise, and in the mountain ranges of the north and east, where the air must rise again. Elsewhere, the park is in a rain shadow and annual precipitation is lower. Most of the park receives between 30 and 50 inches, depending on elevation. Near North Entrance at the park's lowest elevation annual precipitation is only 10 to 12 inches.

Because of the long winters and cool temperatures, much of the precipitation falls as snow. Nearly 50 percent of the total annual precipitation is in the snowpack on the first of April and is released into the soil and the surface waters over the next three months. Rainfall is insufficient to replace water evaporated from the soil surface or drawn from the soil by plants, causing the soils to dry out during the summer. In years of low winter precipitation, drought conditions usually prevail.

The central part of the park is underlain by rhyolitic volcanic rocks laid down between 2 million and 76,000 years ago. Most of the rest of Yellowstone is underlain by andesitic volcanic rocks laid down about 70 million to 80 million years ago. During the Ice Age (lasting from 2 million to about 14,000 years ago), the park was under an ice cap several times. Soils that developed on the two distinct rock types differ in mineral nutrient content and water-holding capacity, both factors of primary importance to plants.

Because the park land was set aside for preservation before many settlers moved into the area, the vegetation has not been manipulated by modern humans to any great extent. In the early days, there was some logging to build the hotels and administrative buildings and some wood-gathering for fuel, but these activities involved relatively small sections of land near the developed areas and roads. Wood-gathering for campfires is still permitted but occurs only near campgrounds and roadways. Cattle and horses were pastured in some areas near the developments, but their stay was brief and ended shortly after the turn of the century. Populations of large wild animals were reduced for a time, but now their numbers, except those of wolves and antelope, appear to have returned to something approximating natural levels. Attempts to control epidemic levels of forest insects were made on two occasions, once for mountain pine beetles and once for spruce budworm, but such insects are now recognized as part of the natural ecosystem. Even lightning-caused fires have been accepted as part of the nature of Yellowstone and are allowed, as much as possible, to play their role in the scheme of things.

Perhaps the greatest influence of modern humans on the vegetation of Yellowstone has been the introduction of new plant species. Timothy and Kentucky bluegrasses are widespread due to the use of horses, and Canada thistle appears to be present wherever it can grow. In all, 97 introduced species have been found so far. The majority are restricted to the lower elevations near the North Entrance where the climate is similar to those of Europe and the Middle East, the origins of most of the exotics.

For the rest of the park, factors that interact with the native vegetation have remained intact and are allowed to influence which plants occur on any particular site. Thus, many interactions are available for study. The park can also act as a benchmark against which nonpark ecosystems can be measured and the full extent of human impact can be assessed.

Knowledge of the vegetation can be very useful in day-to-day management of the park. A major park goal is to eliminate or compensate for human disturbance to maintain, insofar as possible, a natural ecosystem. The vegetation of a particular site can indicate the type of natural environment or how far the site has been displaced from natural conditions. Appropriate revegetation efforts following needed construction or emplacement of utility lines require knowledge of the preconstruction vegetation if they are to succeed.

Finally, vegetation acts as a continuous environmental monitor. If human activity significantly alters environmental conditions, the results will be reflected in plant communities. By watching the vegetation carefully, we should be able to detect changes soon enough to take needed management action.

Definitions

Some words, such as *vegetation,* have technical meanings as well as more common ones, and others, such as *habitat type* and *cover type,* are unfamiliar to many people. The following definitions are used throughout this book.

Plant Communities and Vegetation

Casual inspection reveals that several species of plants grow together on any particular site. Some are tall and some are short; some grow on the ground and some grow on other plants. Some need bright sunlight while others do well in the shade. Some have large, beautiful flowers while others appear to have none. Some have large leaves and some have very tiny leaves or none at all. Some are spherical, others columnar. But always there is variety, and this variety makes possible the division of resources that allows many species to grow together on the same site. A group of plants growing together is called a plant community. Closer examination shows that these communities do not occur at random, but according to consistent and predictable patterns. When in dry places, for example, we find plants seen in other dry places, and when in wet places, we find plants seen in other wet places.

A wide variety of textures, patterns, colors, and even shades of colors make up the various pieces of the vegetative quilt. Just as there are many different shades of red, there are subtle differences between communities belonging to the same class. These shades of difference change not only from place to place but also from one time to another. If we watch a burned forest, for example, over a period of decades or centuries, an orderly succession of plant communities occupies the site until a point is reached where change is no longer noticeable and each succeeding generation of the community is much like its predecessor. Such a community is called a climax community, and the various communities leading up to it are called seral communities. Yellowstone National Park sustains many different plant communities. This collection of plant communities constitutes the vegetation of the park, a rich tapestry woven of the many colors and textures provided by a large variety of plants.

Several systems have been developed to classify plant communities. Some emphasize the communities that would exist on a site after plant succession has produced a stable climax community. Others emphasize the community that is currently growing on the site. Neither approach is used in this book; instead, a dual system is used. Each plant community is classified according to two different criteria: one classifies the physical environment into units called habitat types and the other classifies community development since the last major disturbance into units called cover types.

Habitat Types

Each piece of ground on the earth's surface exists not only in the familiar three dimensions of physical space (length, width, and height) but also in a multidimensional environmental space. This environmental space has the dimensions of temperature, moisture, light, mineral nutrient availability, disturbance frequency, and many other vectors. Sites that are very close together in environmental space may be grouped into units (types) that share a set of common characteristics.

It is sometimes obvious that one particular physical factor such as soil moisture is responsible for the uniqueness of a type, but more often the reason is not so easy to recognize. Most of the time a type is different because of a unique combination of factors (its position in environmental space) rather than because of a single factor. It is impossible to measure all the different environmental factors at a given site; therefore, some indirect method is needed to assess different positions in environmental space. Plant species are long-time residents of a site, especially suited to indicate that site's location in environmental space because they integrate all the environmental factors as well as the interactions among factors.

Ecological requirements of plant species vary. Some have narrow tolerance limits to a particular environmental factor such as moisture or temperature, while other species occur over a very broad range of that factor. The plants with narrow tolerance limits can be used as indicators of the occurrence of those particular conditions. Thus the plant community is a good indirect indicator of a site's position in environmental space.

This integration of the environment by plants is the basis of a classification system developed more than 30 years ago in eastern Washington and western Idaho (1). Since that time, the system has been refined and applied to a large portion of the Rocky Mountain vegetation (2). The units of this system are called habitat types (3). A habitat type is a set of environmental conditions that appears repeatedly across a landscape. An example would be all the south-facing slopes on loamy soils between 7,000 and 8,000 feet elevation. These sites would occupy a different place in environmental space from the south-facing slopes on sandy soils. The plant communities that develop on each habitat type would be different, and these distinct communities can be used to distinguish the two habitat types. This classification lends itself to a hierarchical system. Habitat types can be split into finer divisions, called phases, or combined with similar types into larger groups, called series. For example, all the habitat types dominated by subalpine fir form one series and all those dominated by Douglas-fir form another series.

Habitat types are named after the climax plant community that would develop on that site after sufficient passage of time. Two species are used in the name. The first is a species with broad ecological tolerance that dominates the climax community, for example, subalpine fir or Idaho fescue. The second is a species with more specific requirements that indicates the particular place in environmental space that the habitat type occupies. The first species is also used as the series name. The name of a phase is the habitat type name extended by a third species that is another indicator species. For example, the sticky geranium phase of the Idaho fescue/

bearded wheatgrass habitat type is a grassland belonging to the Idaho fescue series. Idaho fescue tends to occur on cool, moist sites with deep soils; bearded wheatgrass grows well in the middle of the range of sites where Idaho fescue grows; and sticky geranium grows on the most productive sites within this group. Where it is too dry for bearded wheatgrass, bluebunch wheatgrass does well; these sites belong to the Idaho fescue/bluebunch wheatgrass habitat type. On the other hand, where it is too wet for bearded wheatgrass, tufted hairgrass can grow; these sites belong to the Idaho fescue/tufted hairgrass habitat type.

Although the habitat type system is based on climax or near-climax communities, stands of younger age can be classified by observing the species and noting whether they are predominately climax or seral species. For example, a site may be covered by lodgepole pine trees, but if there are more than five subalpine fir per acre among the young trees it is safe to say that the site belongs to the subalpine fir series. Indicators of the specific habitat type usually establish soon after a disturbance, so in most cases the habitat type can be determined.

Cover Types

Following a major disturbance such as fire, vegetation progresses through a series of plant communities (seral communities) toward the climax community. This process is called succession. Succession is a continuous process, but it can be divided into classes (4). Logical divisions would be early, mid, and late stages. Adding recently disturbed and climax stages provides five easily recognizable and ecologically meaningful classes. These classes are called cover types in this book. To date, only the cover types of forested vegetation have been worked out. The major tree species are readily discernible on aerial photographs and different age classes are fairly easy to distinguish, allowing large areas to be mapped quickly and economically.

A disturbance that restarts the successional process is usually widespread enough to include stands of more than one habitat type. Thus, a large area of a particular habitat type may have several different cover types, and a cover type may spread across several habitat types. For example, some of the large rhyolite plateaus in the central part of Yellowstone may contain a habitat type that covers several hundred acres. A fire may burn only a part of that habitat type, so that type would then have at least two cover types: one in the burned areas and another in the nonburned areas. If that same fire burned across a second habitat type, e.g., a seep area, then the same cover type that resulted from the fire would occupy at least two habitat types.

PART ONE
Description of the Habitat Types and Cover Types

Habitat Types

This section delineates the plant communities that develop on the habitat types found in Yellowstone National Park. Most of the information is contained in tables that accompany each habitat type section, to facilitate comparison between the types. Each type represented by more than 1,000 acres in the park is illustrated by two photographs—one showing an overall view and one showing the major indicator species—and a map showing the distribution of that type in the park. With each set of pictures is a short narrative explaining the relationship of the habitat type to fire and other miscellaneous information. The following section serves as a reference for those who wish to get better acquainted with the habitat types or are interested in a particular aspect of a type.

Two major factors determining distribution of habitat types across the landscape are moisture and temperature. The general relationship of habitat types to these factors can be shown in two-dimensional diagrams with moisture along one axis and temperature (which is largely determined by elevation) along the other (Fig. 1). The forested habitat types are shown as they are distributed on the two major rock types that cover the majority of the park. Rock type influences several soil characteristics and is important in determining vegetation distribution in Yellowstone. This is more fully explained in Chapter 5. Interrelations of the physical environment with the types and their distribution on the landscape are discussed in Part Two. Scientific names of the plants are found in Appendix I.

Fire is an important environmental factor in the forested habitat types and in many of those dominated by sagebrush. Fire behavior and return interval are largely determined by fuel accumulation. (Return interval is the amount of time between successive fires on

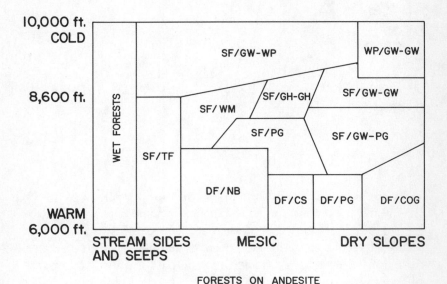

Figure 1A. Forests on andesite

Figure 1. Distribution of habitat types along moisture and elevational gradients

BB = bitterbrush; BBW = bluebunch wheatgrass; BS = big sagebrush; BW = bearded wheatgrass; COG = creeping Oregon grape; CS = common snowberry; DF = Douglas-fir; ES = elk sedge; GH = globe huckleberry; GW = grouse whortleberry; IF = Idaho fescue; LP = lodgepole pine; NB = ninebark; NT = needle-and-thread; PG = pinegrass; RN = Richardson's needlegrass; RS = Ross's sedge; S = sedges; SB = Sandberg's bluegrass; SF = subalpine fir; SG = sticky geranium; SS = silver sagebrush; TF = twinflower; TH = tufted hairgrass; WM = western meadowrue; WP = whitebark pine

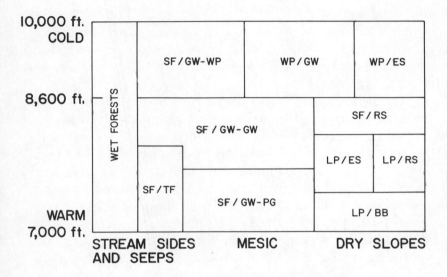

FORESTS ON RHYOLITE

Figure 1B. Forests on rhyolite

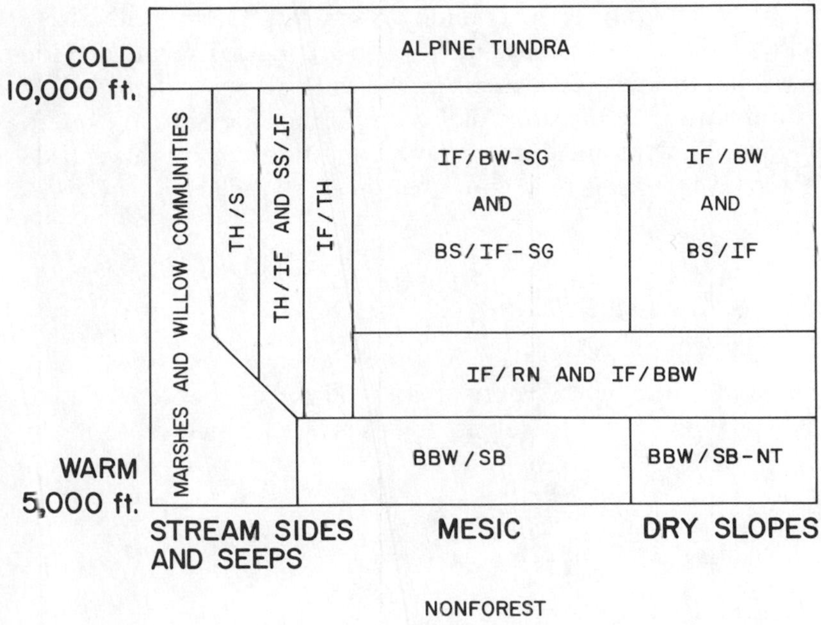

NONFOREST

Figure 1C. Nonforest types

the same site.) Fuel accumulation is determined by the productivity of the site, the rate at which dead plant material is decomposed, and the amount of time available for accumulation. Habitat types differ from one another in the first two parameters while cover types differ in the third.

Several terms commonly used to describe fire behavior may be unfamiliar to most people. Fires that burn the fuels on the surface of the ground are called surface fires while those that burn the tree crowns are called crown fires (such a fire is said to be crowning). If a single tree bursts into flame it is said to be torching. Firebrands, burning bits of small branches, lichens, or needles, are carried upward in the smoke column and fall out on the ground at various distances from the fire. If these firebrands are still hot enough to ignite other fuels when they reach the ground, a small spot begins to burn in the forest floor. If fuel conditions are right, these spots can spread into the crowns. This process is called spotting, and it is the most common method of fire spread when a fire is crowning, allowing a fire to cover large areas in a short time. The smoke column is usually tipped by the wind and most of the firebrands fall out of the column downwind. Occasionally, large billows in the smoke column will drop firebrands upwind and the fire will spot upwind. Sometimes the wind blows toward a higher mountain where the slope of the land brings the ground close to the smoke column. Under these conditions, spots have been observed to start a mile and a half from the main fire.

Forested Habitat Types

About 80 percent of Yellowstone National Park is covered by forested habitat types. Approximately 60 percent of these forested habitat types are in the subalpine fir series, in which subalpine fir dominates the climax communities and lodgepole pine is the dominant seral species (the species that dominates a community developing toward climax).

Wet Forested Habitat Types

Wet forested habitat types occur throughout the park and cover about 8 percent of the park's land. One of the main factors determining their distribution is the nature of rhyolite flows. The rhyolitic flows are quite porous, and a great deal of water percolates through them. The water emerges where the flow contacts the bedrock below, producing a fringe of wet, boggy areas all along the margins of these flows.

Water also collects in depressions on the surface of the rhyolite flows. These depressions have accumulated a layer of fine soil and often have an ephemeral or permanent pond in the center with a ring of wet forest. On the Absaroka volcanics, springs and seeps are less common, but where they occur these wet habitat types are present.

The overstory and understory are dominated by subalpine fir and Engelmann spruce. The forest floor is usually wet, dominated by a variety of wet-site species including horsetails, bluejoint reedgrass, trapper's tea, twisted-stalk, arrowleaf groundsel, and a variety of wet-site mosses. Seral stands usually have a good representation of Engelmann spruce and lodgepole pine.

Minor Forested Habitat Types

The minor forested types are not illustrated by photographs but are included here for those who find themselves in a forest that does not fit the descriptions presented previously. These are minor forested types of limited areal extent or types that occur in a very local part of the park. Most are types that are more abundant in areas adjacent to the park.

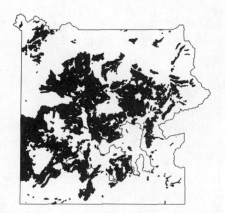

Figure 2. Subalpine fir/grouse whortleberry habitat type, grouse whortleberry phase

This type is one of the most widespread forest habitat types in the Rocky Mountains, yet it is remarkably similar throughout its range. It covers most of the park's middle elevations, accounting for 52 percent of the park's forested area, as shown in the map. Subalpine fir is the climax species (seen scattered throughout Fig. 2A), but stands dominated by subalpine fir are quite rare due to the burnable nature of the late seral stages and the poor growing conditions in much of the area. Grouse whortleberry (Fig. 2B) is usually the only shrub present and often forms a continuous cover. It is a short (6–8 inches) semishrub with green stems. There are three phases in the park. The grouse whortleberry phase, shown in Figure 2A, is most common, accounting for more than a third of the forest area. Much of the area covered by this phase is dry enough that lodgepole pine becomes a long-persisting seral stage and is common in the understory even in stands that are more than 300 years old. The pinegrass phase (not illustrated) is similar in appearance with the addition of pinegrass. In open seral stands of this phase, the grass may even obscure the grouse whortleberry.

Crown fire is common in the later stages of the grouse whortleberry phase (return interval 150–300 years), especially in the more moist portions where spruce and fir reproduce well and grow quickly. Young or middle-aged stands lack understory fuels to carry a fire well, and these stands usually do not burn. Occasionally, forest floor vegetation is dense enough to carry fire and surface fires of a few tens of acres may occur. These fires spread slowly because wind cannot penetrate the canopy. The droughty soils dry early, so these stands do not require as dry a season as other habitat types to reach a flammable state.

Figure 2A

Figure 2B

Figure 3. Subalpine fir/grouse whortleberry habitat type, whitebark pine phase

This phase is the colder upper-elevation phase of the habitat type, occurring above 8,600 feet elevation in the areas shown in the map. Older stands are usually open, allowing whitebark pine to persist in the community (Fig. 3A). Engelmann spruce and subalpine fir are usually present in all seral stages. Grouse whortleberry forms a continuous cover (Fig. 3B). This phase is especially important to grizzly bears because the seral stages provide abundant pine-nut crops. The bears must wait until squirrels harvest the cones from the trees, and this phase contains enough other tree species that the squirrels can survive years when whitebark pine do not produce many seeds. Whitebark pine habitat types usually do not have this feature, and although they produce abundant seed, the squirrels are not present to harvest the cones for the bears.

Fires are uncommon in this phase because of their higher, cooler location. Fire return intervals are long (300–400 years). Under very dry and windy conditions they burn both as crown fires and surface fires but such years are rare.

Figure 3A

Figure 3B

Figure 4. Subalpine fir/globe huckleberry habitat type

The subalpine fir/globe huckleberry type has a lush understory (Fig. 4A) with a high diversity of herbaceous and shrubby species on the forest floor. Globe huckleberry (shown in Fig. 4B) occasionally produces berries, but most years the climate is just too marginal for berry production. Two phases occur in the park in the areas shown in the map. The grouse whortleberry phase is a cool, often drier phase with less diversity and lower biomass on the forest floor. The globe huckleberry phase (shown in Figures 4A and 4B) grows on the warmer, lower elevations of the type and is more diverse, especially with shrubby species.

Fuels are abundant in this type and even middle-aged stands can have enough understory fuel to support crown fire even before spruce and fir are common in the understory. The fire season must be quite dry before these stands will burn well. Fire return intervals are moderate (200–300 years). Dry years are required before the lush understory will burn. When they do, large crown fires can burn several hundred acres in an afternoon.

Figure 4A

Figure 4B

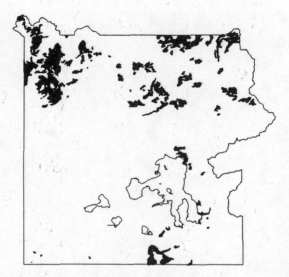

Figure 5. Subalpine fir/western meadowrue habitat type

Subalpine fir/western meadowrue stands usually have a lush forest floor vegetation composed mainly of forbs, although several shrub species may be present. Figure 5B shows the broadleaved showy aster growing with western meadowrue. Subalpine fir regeneration is usually dense under older stands (Fig. 5A). Douglas-fir or whitebark pine, as well as the ever-present lodgepole pine, may dominate the seral stands The map shows where this habitat type occurs.

Fire return intervals are moderate (200–300 years). Dry years are required before the lush understory will burn. When they do, large crown fires can burn several hundred acres in an afternoon.

Figure 5A

Figure 5B

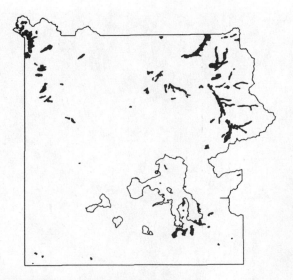

Figure 6. Subalpine fir/twinflower habitat type

The twinflower type occurs in slightly moist areas along benches, flood plains, and lower slopes throughout the park (as shown in the map), but is most common on andesitic volcanic rocks. Engelmann spruce is more common and persistent in this type than in other types and co-dominates with subalpine fir in the climax and other late seral stands. Twinflower (shown in Fig. 6B) is usually inconspicuous below the other forest floor plants. There are two phases in the park. The most common one is the grouse whortleberry phase, which is dominated by grouse whortleberry. The twinflower phase has less grouse whortleberry but may have other shrubs. Even mid-succession stages have a good representation of Engelmann spruce and subalpine fir, as seen in Figure 6A.

Fire return intervals are moderate (200–300 years). Fairly dry summers are needed to dry the fuels sufficiently to burn well. However, when they do dry out, crown fire is easily propagated through these stands. Good growth of both spruce and subalpine fir provides abundant understory fuels within 200 years or less.

Figure 6A

Figure 6B

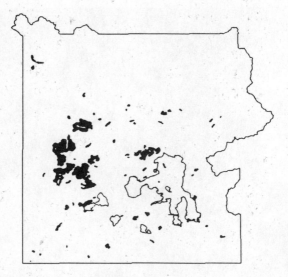

Figure 7. Subalpine fir/elk sedge habitat type

The subalpine fir/elk sedge type is one of the dry infertile types but has sufficient moisture for at least slow growth of subalpine fir. This type occurs in that areas shown in the map. The forest floor is rather sparse and dominated by clumps of elk sedge (shown in Fig. 7B). This sedge is recognized by the single seed on the seed stalk. Shrubs are scarce. The stands are usually quite open and lodgepole pine are also dominant in the understory even in near climax stands, as seen in Figure 7A.

Fire return intervals are long (300–400 years) because of the slow growth rates, lack of understory fuels, and sparse overstory. It will burn, however the fires are quite spotty. Patches of seedlings and saplings will produce crown fires, but sparser areas will be skipped.

Figure 7A

Figure 7B

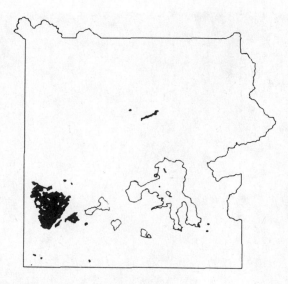

Figure 8. Subalpine fir/Ross's sedge habitat type

The map indicates areas of the subalpine fir/Ross's sedge type, which is a dry, cool, infertile type. The stands are quite open and the forest floor vegetation very sparse, as seen in Figure 8A. There is a lot of unvegetated ground covered with pine needle litter. Enough moisture is present to support some subalpine fir but grouse whortleberry is rare to absent. Even in older stands (shown in Fig. 8A), lodgepole pine is very common in both the understory and overstory. Reproduction of both subalpine fir and lodgepole pine grow in patches. These sites grade into a lodgepole pine/Ross's sedge habitat type where the environment is drier. The soils are very coarse and do not hold much soil moisture. Spring snowmelt mostly runs off or drops through the rooting zone. The forest floor is quite sparse with widely scattered clumps of Ross's sedge (shown in Fig. 8B) scattered around.

Fire return intervals are rather long (400 years or more), and fires are very spotty due to the patchy nature of the reproduction. Firebrands from a fire must be blown some distance if the fires are to attain many acres in these areas.

Figure 8A

Figure 8B

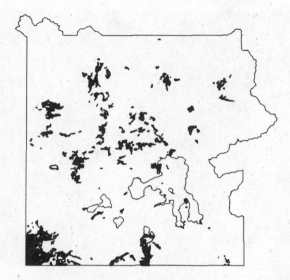

Figure 9. Subalpine fir/pinegrass habitat type

Subalpine fir/pinegrass types are on warmer, more fertile sites (shown in the map) than the other types. The forest floor is usually a sward of pinegrass and elk sedge (Fig. 9B), even in stands older than that shown in Figure 9A. Engelmann spruce is usually present and Douglas-fir can often be found. In some cases, Douglas-fir may be a major component of the seral stages.

Fire return intervals are moderate (200–300 years) because of the slower establishment and growth of subalpine fir and spruce. The pinegrass will dry out in the fall of dry years and is capable of carrying extensive surface fires even in young to middle-aged lodgepole pine. This is one of the very few types in the park that will support this type of fire behavior.

Figure 9A

Figure 9B

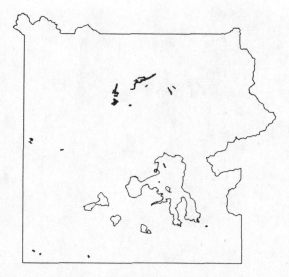

Figure 10. Lodgepole pine/Ross's sedge habitat type

Some sites (indicated in the map) are too dry for subalpine fir but will support lodgepole pine. The lodgepole pine are widely spaced, and reproduction is stunted and infrequent (as seen in Fig. 10A). Subalpine fir is occasionally found in favorable microsites. Forest floor vegetation is very sparse, consisting mostly of widely scattered clumps of Ross's sedge (shown in Fig. 10B) and Oregon grape. This type is not recognized by others who have worked in this area (1, 2, 4) but is considered a lodgepole pine community type.

Fire is infrequent and spotty in this type (return interval 400–600 years). Fuels are produced slowly. Fire rarely starts in this type and spread is very difficult. Fires burning into these stands from other stands stop. Firebrands burn some of the rotten logs, but few if any trees are killed.

Figure 10A

Figure 10B

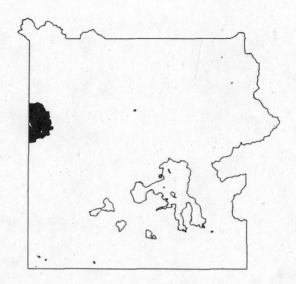

Figure 11. Lodgepole pine/bitterbrush habitat type

The lodgepole pine/bitterbrush type ranges from a nearly continuous stand with occasional bitterbrush openings to islands of lodgepole pine in a bitterbrush matrix. This type occurs in the park only in the specific area shown in the map. Lodgepole pine grow only 15 to 30 feet high and reproduction is rare (as shown in Fig. 11A). The bitterbrush is only 1 to 2 feet high (Fig. 11B) and the grasses are sparse. The soils are derived from outwash sands and gravel and are very poor and dry.

Fuels are produced very slowly after a fire so the return intervals are long (400–600 years). Older, more productive sites may burn large areas while fires in the other sites are more spotty.

Figure 11A

Figure 11B

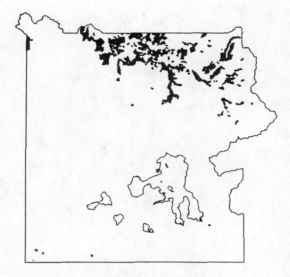

Figure 12. Douglas-fir/common snowberry habitat type

The Douglas-fir/common snowberry type is intermixed in the sage-brush types in the areas shown in the map. Common snowberry is quite abundant in the earlier stages but thins out as the crowns shade the forest floor. Pinegrass may form a layer beneath the snowberry (seen in Fig. 12B). These stands are quite diverse with many species of shrubs and forbs. The overstory is a mixture of very old trees and intermediate-sized trees (Fig. 12A). Very few if any small trees and tree reproduction are found in these stands. See the discussion in Chapter 7 in the section on plant succession.

Fire return intervals probably were 50 to 100 years or less. The lower elevations, warmer climate, and productive forest floor and understory provide for frequent surface fires. One study on the fire frequency in the northern part of the park indicated that these stands may have burned as frequently as every 20 to 30 years (3). Fire suppression has prevented these site from burning for one to two cycles, and some fuel accumulation may have resulted especially in the form of young Douglas-fir. A recent outbreak of spruce budworm has eliminated a number of these younger trees and thinned the older ones. This outbreak may have accomplished what natural fires would have had they not been suppressed.

Figure 2A

Figure 12B

Figure 13. Douglas-fir/pinegrass habitat type

Douglas-fir is the most common seral dominant as well as the climax forest tree in this type, although lodgepole pine may very occasionally form a seral stand. This type occurs in the various areas shown in the map. The forest floor is usually a sward of pinegrass and forb species, as seen in Figure 13A. Shrubs are widely scattered. As the forest matures and becomes more shaded, the forest floor thins out. Pinegrass often grows to a foot or more in length as shown in Figure 13B. It very rarely flowers unless it is burned; then it flowers and sets seed profusely.

Fire return intervals are now moderately long but could have been very short in earlier times. (See the fire discussion under Douglas-fir/common snowberry habitat type.) Live Douglas-fir needles are slow to ignite and crown fire is rare; however, the pinegrass could support a surface fire quite well late in dry years.

Figure 13A

Figure 13B

Figure 14. Douglas-fir/mallow ninebark habitat type

Douglas-fir dominates both seral and climax stands of the Douglas-fir/mallow ninebark type. This is the only plant community with a well-developed shrub layer, as shown in Figure 14A. The mallow ninebark is only 2 to 3 feet high but quite dense. These stands are nearly confined to steep north-facing slopes at lower elevations (shown in the map). Mallow ninebark is recognized by the three to five lobed, coarsely veined leaves and clusters of small white flowers, as shown in Figure 14B. The bark on older stems appears to be peeling off in long strips.

The fire return intervals are probably longer in the Douglas-fir/mallow ninebark type because of the cooler, more moist site conditions. However, mallow ninebark is usually so dense that crown fires are more common in this type than in other Douglas-fir types.

Figure 14A

Figure 14B

Figure 15. Whitebark pine/grouse whortleberry habitat type

The whitebark pine/grouse whortleberry type is rather open in the later stages of succession. Grouse whortleberry (shown in Fig. 15B) forms a nearly continuous stand on the forest floor. The stand shown in Figure 15A is more dense and has more subalpine fir than is typical of this type. Lodgepole pine is restricted to the lower elevations of this type but may persist to be a part of the climax forest. At upper elevations, whitebark pine is both seral and climax dominant. The map indicates where this type occurs.

Although these stands produce abundant pine-nut crops occasionally, the grizzly bears seldom use them for food. These stands lack enough other conifers to provide squirrels with an alternate food source during non-pine-nut years; consequently, there are no squirrels to cut the cones down for the bears. The bears do, however, feed on the inner bark at the base of the trees and produce scars that are indistinguishable from fire scars after a few years.

Large fires are infrequent due to the high elevations and lack of under-story fuels. The stands seldom dry sufficiently to burn, but following dry winters where snowfall is less than about 60 percent of normal, the stands will burn if summer weather is dry.

Figure 15A

Figure 15B

Figure 16. Wet forested habitat types

Three habitat types occupy most of the forested wet sites (shown in the map). The Engelmann spruce/common horsetail habitat type and the Engelmann spruce/sweetscented bedstraw habitat type are more common on the andesitic areas of the park. The subalpine fir/bluejoint reedgrass type (shown in Figures 16A and 16B) is more common where rhyolite is the dominant bedrock. These stands occur on flood plains and seep areas throughout the park. Bluejoint reedgrass forms a thick sward of grass often reaching 18 inches to 2 feet in length, as shown in both Figures 16A and 16B.

Fire return intervals are moderate in these stands. Older stands have an abundance of fuels in the form of young spruce and fir and accumulated grasses and forbs. During very dry years these dead grasses dry out sufficiently to carry a fire and good crown fires are able to develop. Younger stands like those shown in Figures 16A and 16B will carry a good surface fire and lodgepole pine trees in these stands may have two to three fire scars at the base. After a fire burns through stands of these types, the forest floor vegetation resprouts immediately. The heat pulse does not go far into the soil, and the rhizomes and other plant parts are damaged little if at all. The grass species begin to grow new leaves within a few days, and together with the other species, soon produce dense groundcover. Engelmann spruce and subalpine fir are common among the young trees as a forest develops on these sites.

Figure 16A

Figure 16B

TABLE 1
Characteristics of major forested habitat types (indicator species and dominant species are in capital letters)

Phase	Distribution*	Altitude (feet)	Common species	Soil condition
Subalpine fir/grouse whortleberry habitat type pinegrass phase	Especially abundant in the western portion of the Central Plateaus; occurs on warmer, slightly more fertile areas in western and northern parts of the park; occupies 2% of park	6,500–7,900	Pinegrass, grouse WHORTLEBERRY, early blue violet, sticky geranium, LODGEPOLE PINE	Rhyolitic, infertile, droughty
grouse whortleberry phase	Covers most of the central portion of the park; occupies 36% of park		LODGEPOLE PINE, Douglas-fir, Engelmann spruce, subalpine fir, grouse WHORTLE-BERRY, elk sedge, heartleaf arnica, one-sided wintergreen, mosses, lichens	Rhyolitic, infertile, droughty

47

whitebark pine phase	Occurs at the higher elevations of the Gallatin and Absaroka ranges; occupies 14% of the park	8,500–9,800	WHITEBARK PINE, subalpine fir, Engelmann spruce, lodgepole pine, grouse whortleberry, showy aster, Engelmann aster, Ross's sedge, fireweed	Andesitic, more fertile and more moist than other phases
Subalpine fir/globe huckleberry habitat type	Extensively distributed throughout the Absaroka Range and lower, wetter portions of the Southwest Plateaus (Bechler); occasionally in the Gallatin Range; occupies 8% of park	7,100–8,700	LODGEPOLE PINE, ENGELMANN SPRUCE, SUBALPINE FIR, GLOBE HUCKLEBERRY, Utah honeysuckle, Engelmann aster, Cascade mountain-ash, pinegrass, elk sedge, heartleaf arnica, one-sided wintergreen, showy aster, Ross's sedge	Derived from andesitic till except in Southwest Plateaus, where derived from basaltic bedrock; rich with good water-holding capacity

TABLE 1
(continued)

Phase	Distribution*	Altitude (feet)	Common species	Soil condition
Subalpine fir/western meadowrue habitat type	Common in the Gallatin Range; sporadic throughout the Absaroka Range; occupies gentle to moderately steep terrain on various aspects	7,600–8,900	LODGEPOLE PINE, SUBALPINE FIR, ENGELMANN SPRUCE, occasionally DOUGLAS-FIR, whitebark pine, mountain sweetroot, heartleaf arnica, pinegrass, fireweed, WESTERN MEADOWRUE, mountain gooseberry	Andesitic till, sedimentary rock, good fertility and soil moisture
Subalpine fir/twinflower habitat type twinflower phase	Commonly along toe slopes of many valleys in the Gallatin and Absaroka ranges and other moister areas; not common in park		LODGEPOLE PINE, ENGELMANN SPRUCE, SUBALPINE FIR, Douglas-fir, HEARTLEAF ARNICA, Utah honeysuckle, GROUSE WHORTLE-	Andesitic, fairly fertile; wet

	Elevation and vegetation	Soils	Distribution and occurrence
	BERRY, TWIN-FLOWER, fireweed, raceme pussytoes, one-sided wintergreen		
grouse whortleberry phase	7,100–8,000 GROUSE WHORTLE-BERRY, Utah honeysuckle, creeping Oregon grape, russet buffalo berry, prickly rose	Rhyolitic or rhyolitic mixed with lake sediments or andesitic rocks; wet	More common than twinflower phase; occurs on gentle slopes and benches as well as toe slopes; occupies 2% of park
Subalpine fir/elk sedge habitat type	7,800–8,600 LODGEPOLE PINE, Engelmann spruce, subalpine fir, ELK SEDGE, mountain sweetroot, heartleaf arnica, pinegrass, fireweed, western meadowrue, mountain gooseberry; whitebark pine is sporadic but increasingly abundant in higher elevations	Rhyolitic till, coarse, well drained; dry	Occurs mostly along the eastern edge of the Southwest Plateaus; scattered throughout the Central Plateaus; occupies 3% of park

50

TABLE 1
(continued)

Phase	Distribution*	Altitude (feet)	Common species	Soil condition
Subalpine fir/Ross's sedge habitat type	Occurs mainly on the Madison Plateau on a variety of aspects and slopes; occupies 2% of park	8,000–9,000	LODGEPOLE PINE, ROSS'S SEDGE, heartleaf arnica, yarrow, mountain sweetroot, SUBALPINE FIR	Rhyolitic, coarse, dry, poor in mineral nutrients; some are influenced by windblown material mixed in upper horizons
Subalpine fir/pinegrass habitat type	Occurs extensively in the Bechler area, occasionally in the Central Plateaus; occupies a variety of aspects on gentle to moderate slopes; occupies 5% of park	6,400–7,000	LODGEPOLE PINE, DOUGLAS-FIR, SUBALPINE FIR, PINEGRASS, ELK SEDGE, Engelmann spruce, heartleaf arnica, sticky geranium, asters, serviceberry, mountain snowberry, early blue violet, white-flowered hawkweed	Rhyolitic; influenced by loess or andesitic till; coarse, moderately dry
Lodgepole pine/Ross's sedge habitat type	Occurs on steep south-facing slopes; occupies less than 1% of park	7,000–8,000	LODGEPOLE PINE, silvery lupine, northern goldenrod, lanceleaf	Rhyolitic, infertile, dry

Habitat type	Elevation (feet)	Distribution and comments	Dominant vegetation	Substrate
Lodgepole pine/elk sedge habitat type	7,000–8,000	Occurs on steep south-facing slopes; occupies less than 1% of park	LODGEPOLE PINE, whitebark pine, ELK SEDGE, silvery lupine stonecrop, ROSS'S SEDGE, Wheeler's bluegrass	Rhyolitic, infertile, dry
Lodgepole pine/bitterbrush habitat type	6,600–6,800	Occupies a large outwash gravel plain near West Yellowstone, Montana	LODGEPOLE PINE, whitebark pine, BITTERBRUSH, Idaho fescue, timber oatgrass, Ross's sedge, rosy pussytoes, ballhead sandwort, many-flowered phlox	Rhyolitic sand and gravel, poor in nutrients; very dry; low amounts of silt and clay
Douglas-fir/common snowberry habitat type	6,000–7,400	Yellowstone and Lamar River Valleys on warmer sites; lower slopes and benches with relatively mild climates; deep moist soils and northern to eastern aspects; occurs on 3% of park	ASPEN, LODGEPOLE PINE, DOUGLAS-FIR, COMMON SNOWBERRY, shiny-leaf spirea, creeping Oregon grape, chokecherry, serviceberry, pinegrass, western yarrow, false Solomon's seal	Glacial till derived from nonacidic volcanic rocks such as basalt and andesite and sedimentary rocks such as limestone and sandstones

TABLE 1
(continued)

Phase	Distribution*	Altitude (feet)	Common species	Soil condition
Douglas-fir/pinegrass habitat type	Most common in the Yellowstone-Lamar valleys in areas that appear to be too cold for common snowberry but still warm enough for pinegrass; usually occupies upper slopes; occurs on 2% of park	6,000–7,600	DOUGLAS-FIR, aspen, lodgepole pine, PINE-GRASS, yarrow, heart-leaf arnica, woods strawberry, sticky geranium, shiny-leaf spirea	Derived from andesitic and sedimentary till; sometimes rhyolite is also a major component; mesic moisture status
Douglas-fir/shiny-leaf spirea habitat type	Occurs almost entirely in the Yellowstone-Lamar River Valleys; occupies upper slopes and ridges having various aspects; occurs on less than 1% of park	6,600–8,200	DOUGLAS-FIR, SHINY-LEAF SPIREA, OREGON BOXWOOD, serviceberry, mountain snowberry, creeping Oregon grape, Wheeler's bluegrass, yarrow, heart-leaf arnica, weedy milk-vetch	Derived from dry, andesitic and sedimentary tills
Douglas-fir/mallow ninebark habitat type	Common in the Yellowstone-Lamar River Valleys but not	6,000–7,500	DOUGLAS-FIR, aspen, MALLOW NINE-BARK, shiny-leaf	Derived from andesitic, Derived from andesitic and sedimentary tills;

Habitat type	Occurrence	Elevation	Dominant vegetation	Soil
	common in rest of park; occurs on very steep northern aspects and other moist, protected slopes; occupies less than 1% of park		spirea, russet buffalo berry, heartleaf arnica, showy aster, weedy milkvetch, wild strawberry	colluvial slopes are quite rocky; nutrients and water-holding capacity are usually high
Whitebark pine/grouse whortleberry habitat type	Found near timberline along the dry eastern Absaroka Range and in drier parts of high elevations of the Southwest Plateaus; occupies 2% of the park	8,600–10,500	LODGEPOLE PINE, WHITEBARK PINE, GROUSE WHORTLEBERRY, Wheeler's bluegrass, Ross's sedge, heartleaf arnica	Derived from andesitic till and bedrock but usually from the drier, coarser types, which produce a dry soil
Whitebark pine/elk sedge habitat type	Occurs at higher elevations in the Central Plateaus and the drier eastern part of the Southwest Plateaus; occupies steep southern to western aspects at somewhat lower elevations on gentle benches and flats; occupies 1% of park	8,600–9,400	WHITEBARK PINE, LODGEPOLE PINE, ELK SEDGE, Idaho fescue, western needlegrass, downy oatgrass, yarrow, heartleaf arnica, harebell, fireweed, northern goldenrod	Derived from rhyolite; coarse and dry

*The park can be divided into five geovegetation provinces: Gallatin Range, Absaroka Range, Central Plateaus, Southwest Plateaus, and Yellowstone-Lamar River Valleys. Descriptions of these provinces are in Chapter 6.

TABLE 2
Characteristics of wet forest habitat types (indicator species and dominant species are in capital letters).

Phase	Distribution*	Altitude (feet)	Common species
Engelmann spruce/common horsetail habitat type	Found along spring-fed drainages and seeps in the Yellowstone–Lamar River Valleys where cold-air drainage allows spruce to grow; occupies the saturated soils of stream terraces, benches, or seeps	6,200–8,700	ENGELMANN SPRUCE, LODGEPOLE PINE, subalpine fir, COMMON HORSETAIL, twisted-stalk, fringed grass-of-parnassus, arrowleaf groundsel, various wet site sedges, rushes, small-flowered woodrush
Engelmann spruce/sweetscented bedstraw habitat type	Not common in the park but has been observed in the north-central part; typically occurs on alluvial terraces or bottomlands; occasionally associated with seeps	6,100–8,200	ENGELMANN SPRUCE, subalpine fir, LODGEPOLE PINE, Douglas-fir, SWEETSCENTED BEDSTRAW, western red baneberry, starry Solomon's seal, TWISTED-STALK, ARROWLEAF GROUNDSEL, BLUEJOINT REEDGRASS

Subalpine fir/bluejoint reedgrass habitat type trapper's tea phase	Incidental phase in the park	7,500–8,800 LODGEPOLE PINE, ENGELMANN SPRUCE, subalpine fir, TRAPPER'S TEA
dwarf huckleberry phase	Incidental phase in the park; usually on poorer sites	7,500–8,000 LODGEPOLE PINE, ENGELMANN SPRUCE, Douglas-fir, subalpine fir, DWARF HUCKLEBERRY
bluejoint reedgrass phase	The typical phase in Yellowstone; common throughout the park; usually appears along stream terraces, pond margins, and at the moist base of slopes	6,800–9,100 LODGEPOLE PINE, ENGELMANN SPRUCE, SUBALPINE FIR, BLUEJOINT REEDGRASS

*The park can be divided into five geovegetation provinces: Gallatin Range, Absaroka Range, Central Plateaus, Southwest Plateaus, and Yellowstone-Lamar River Valleys. Descriptions of these provinces are in Chapter 6.

TABLE 3
Characteristics of minor forested habitat types (indicator species and dominant species are in capital letters)

Phase	Distribution*	Altitude (feet)	Common species	Soil condition
Engelmann spruce/ twinflower habitat type	Occurs in small areas along stream bottoms and lower slopes in the upper part of the Yellowstone-Lamar River Valleys and the lower part of the Absaroka Range; found on steep slopes as well as alluvial terraces and well-drained benches that shed cold air	6,200–8,200	LODGEPOLE PINE, DOUGLAS-FIR, ENGELMANN SPRUCE, TWINFLOWER, common juniper, common snowberry	In the northeast portion of the park the type grows on Absaroka volcanics; relatively rich; moderate to high water-holding capacity
Engelmann spruce/ heartleaf arnica habitat type	Occurs on some drier sites in the Absaroka Range but is much more common south and west of Yellowstone; appears mainly on gentle northwestern to eastern aspects	7,500– 10,000	Andesitic sites: DOUGLAS-FIR, LODGEPOLE PINE, whitebark pine	

		6,700–8,200	
Subalpine fir/baneberry habitat type	Found occasionally in the park on areas that receive some additional moisture; on moist but drained alluvial terraces, lower slopes, and occasionally old landslides		ENGELMANN SPRUCE, SUBALPINE FIR, LODGEPOLE PINE, Douglas-fir, BANEBERRY, Utah honeysuckle, globe huckleberry, thimbleberry, Rocky Mountain maple
Subalpine fir/beargrass habitat type globe huckleberry phase	Incidental habitat type; occurs near the southwest border of the park		LODGEPOLE PINE, DOUGLAS-FIR, Engelmann spruce, GLOBE HUCKLEBERRY, BEARGRASS
grouse whortleberry phase			LODGEPOLE PINE, Engelmann spruce, GROUSE WHORTLEBERRY, BEARGRASS (globe huckleberry sparse)

TABLE 3
(continued)

Phase	Distribution*	Altitude (feet)	Common species	Soil condition
Subalpine fir/mountain arnica habitat type	Small areas appear sporadically; occupies gentle to moderate terrain	7,400–9,300	ENGELMANN SPRUCE, SUBALPINE FIR, Douglas-fir, lodgepole pine, MOUNTAIN GOOSEBERRY, OREGON BOXWOOD, MOUNTAIN ARNICA, Engelmann aster, sickletop lousewort	
Subalpine fir/common snowberry habitat type	Minor habitat type; found mainly in the Snake River Range; observed in the park's southwest corner; occupies benches, lower slopes, and well-drained alluvial terraces	5,700–7,600	LODGEPOLE PINE, DOUGLAS-FIR, Engelmann spruce, aspen, SERVICEBERRY, COMMON SNOWBERRY, pinegrass	

Subalpine fir/Oregon grape habitat type	Observed in the southeast corner of the park; can occupy a variety of sites; most common on moderate slopes having northern aspects	6,600–8,900 DOUGLAS-FIR, Engelmann spruce, ASPEN or LODGEPOLE PINE, subalpine fir, OREGON BOXWOOD, CREEPING OREGON GRAPE, mountain snowberry, russet buffalo berry, serviceberry, HEARTLEAF ARNICA, moss (*Brachythecium collinum*) appears frequently	
Subalpine fir/heartleaf arnica habitat type heartleaf arnica phase	Observed in the northwest corner of the park; found on most aspects; gentle to moderate terrain	7,800–9,600 LODGEPOLE PINE; occasionally Engelmann spruce or Douglas-fir, SUBALPINE FIR, russet buffalo berry, HEARTLEAF ARNICA	Parent materials are mainly sandstone, granite, and quartzite but also include shale, andesite, and occasionally limestone

TABLE 3
(continued)

Phase	Distribution*	Altitude (feet)	Common species	Soil condition
Whitebark pine/common juniper habitat type russet buffalo berry phase	Appears sporadically in southern Absaroka Range on very dry sites	8,000–8,700	LODGEPOLE PINE, WHITEBARK PINE, RUSSET BUFFALO BERRY, WEEDY MILKVETCH, HEARTLEAF ARNICA	
Douglas-fir/common juniper habitat type	Occupies extensive areas of the Absaroka Range; observed in the Yellowstone-Lamar River Valleys; normally occupies exposed rocky slopes at lower to middle elevations of the forest zone	~6,500	DOUGLAS-FIR, limber pine; occasionally lodgepole pine, COMMON JUNIPER, mountain snowberry; russet buffalo berry usually occurs in younger stands; HEARTLEAF ARNICA, WEEDY MILKVETCH	

Habitat type	Elevation	Characteristics	Distribution
Douglas-fir/heartleaf arnica habitat type heartleaf arnica phase	6,900–7,500	Usually DOUGLAS-FIR and small amounts of limber pine are the only trees present; lodgepole pine may appear; undergrowth depauperate; mountain snowberry, Wheeler's bluegrass, Idaho fescue, HEARTLEAF ARNICA, WEEDY MILKVETCH	Major habitat type on the eastern flank of the Absaroka Range; observed in the northeast part of the park; occupies a variety of dry aspects
Douglas-fir/mountain snowberry habitat type	6,600	Trees are usually widely spaced; Douglas-fir is typically only tree on site; occasionally limber pine present; MOUNTAIN SNOWBERRY, big sagebrush, squaw currant, forbs sparse, BLUEBUNCH WHEATGRASS	Observed in the northeast corner of the park; can occupy a variety of slopes and aspects, but southern aspects are most common

*The park can be divided into five geovegetation provinces: Gallatin Range, Absaroka Range, Central Plateaus, Southwest Plateaus, and Yellowstone-Lamar River Valleys. Descriptions of these provinces are in Chapter 6.

Shrub and Grass Habitat Types

Nonforested plant communities occur throughout the park but are most common on areas underlain by andesite and sedimentary rocks. The most extensive nonforested vegetation can be found in the lower elevations of the northern part of the park, which serve as winter range for a large and diverse group of ungulates.

The soils of these areas are much richer, higher in silt and clay, and higher in organic matter than soils derived from rhyolite. On the rhyolitic plateaus, nonforest vegetation seems to be restricted to places where past events have deposited large amounts of fine soil particles. Both Pelican and Hayden valleys have soils that are derived from lake sediments deposited when ice dammed the Yellowstone River during the Ice Age and Yellowstone Lake was up to 300 feet deeper. On Pitchstone Plateau, forest vegetation occurs on the pressure ridges left when the rhyolite flowed out of the ground. The soil on these ridges is rocky and much of the fine soil has washed off the steeper slopes. Between these ridges, a deep layer of wind-deposited fine soil covers the rhyolitic sands and gravels and a grassland has developed.

Fires seldom burn the grasslands and shrublands of the park now. The upper elevation sites are covered with snow or are too wet to burn early and late in the fire season. During the peak of the fire season, they are too green to ignite. The green grass absorbs too much heat in evaporation of water to be able to sustain combustion. Forest fires typically burn up to the edge of the meadows and skip over or go around them.

In the past, the shrublands burned quite frequently (1), and today the dense sagebrush stands burn very well if ignited in the spring before much green grass has grown or in the late fall after the grass has cured. The source of ignition for the frequent fires of the past is not certain. No large forest fires have been allowed to burn near a sagebrush community and lightning has not ignited any fires in sagebrush. Several fires have started in isolated Douglas-fir trees within sagebrush communities but the fires have not spread much beyond the accumulated dead branches and needles below the tree. The possibility exists that past high fire frequency was a result of burning by native peoples who lived in this area.

Miscellaneous Groups and Undescribed Nonforested Habitat Types

The descriptions of the nonforested types have so far been of the most common types that cover significant acreage in Yellowstone. The small scale of the types and the high diversity of types in small areas, especially in alpine and wet areas, means that there can be a wide variety of different types. Interest in these plant communities is just now reaching a point that scientists are beginning to describe the different habitat types. Many types are not yet described, although one study has provided a good description of wetland habitat types in central Yellowstone (2). The following paragraphs describe in a general way some of these types and groups of types.

Sedge marshes and other very wet areas. Sedge marshes, or bogs, and other very wet areas are distributed throughout the park wherever groundwater and topography combine to produce standing water throughout most or all of the growing season.

These very wet areas are dominated by various species of sedges such as water sedge or inflated sedge. Around the fringes of this type, the tufted hairgrass/sedge habitat type and the wet forested habitat type (described above) usually occur.

Willow/sedge habitat types. Willow/sedge types are a very heterogeneous group of wet types dominated by various species of willows. They are distributed along the streams and near many seeps throughout the park. The largest concentration is on the delta of the Yellowstone River where it enters Yellowstone Lake. Large areas of willows also occur along the Gallatin and Madison rivers and along several small creeks throughout the park. Smaller stands are associated with various seep areas.

Sedges and reedgrasses are usually found under the willows. The various species of willow seem to occupy different habitat types, although there is some degree of overlap. Few species are common to most willow stands, but moist-area forbs such as graceful cinquefoil, meadow pussytoes, and western mountain aster are commonly encountered. (*Text resumes on page 94.*)

Figure 17. Bluebunch wheatgrass/Sandberg's bluegrass habitat type

Two phases of the bluebunch wheatgrass/Sandberg's bluegrass type occur in Yellowstone, both of them near the North Entrance at the lowest elevations, as shown in the map. The needle-and-thread phase is dominated by needle-and-thread and has little bluebunch wheatgrass and little to no Sandberg's bluegrass. It occurs mainly on the river deposited sands and gravels. The Sandberg's bluegrass phase, shown in Figures 17A and 17B, occurs on the better soils of the mudflows, has little to no needle-and-thread, and the bluegrass is most commonly found in slightly more moist areas. Bluebunch wheatgrass (shown in Fig. 17B) is most common in this phase. Both phases have rather sparse vegetation and do not produce much forage, especially in dry years. These grasslands are winter ranges for numerous elk and are the only areas where antelope winter.

Figure 17A

Figure 17B

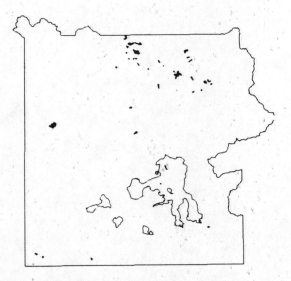

Figure 18. Idaho fescue/bluebunch wheatgrass habitat type

The Idaho fescue/bluebunch wheatgrass type, which occurs on the sites shown in the map, is transitional between the lower bluebunch wheatgrass types and the higher Idaho fescue types. The Idaho fescue is often stunted with leaves 1 to 2 inches long. This type is scattered throughout the Lamar and lower Yellowstone River valleys, usually on windswept ridges. On the winter ranges it is one of the first communities to begin growth in the spring. Both Idaho fescue and bluebunch wheatgrass are shown in Figure 18B. Idaho fescue has dense fine leaves, while bluebunch wheatgrass has fewer and coarser leaves. The stand may have a scattering of shrubs other than sagebrush (Fig. 18A).

Figure 18A

Figure 18B

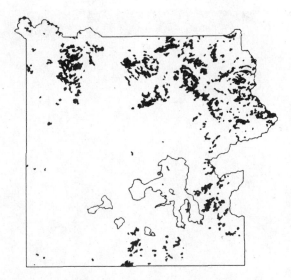

Figure 19. Idaho fescue/bearded wheatgrass habitat type

The Idaho fescue/bearded wheatgrass type is the largest grassland habitat type in the park. It is most common on the andesitic volcanics in the north and east portions of the park, as shown on the map. The sticky geranium phase is highly productive and Idaho fescue usually produces leaves 6 to 8 inches long. This type provides a large portion of the summer range for the park's large animal populations. Even grizzly bears spend a lot of time digging yampa roots in this type. When the site is highly disturbed by pocket gopher and grizzly bear digging, Idaho fescue is rare and large forbs are more common. A dense clump of Idaho fescue is shown in Figure 19B. Figure 19A shows a wetter area surrounded by a more sparse, drier vegetation. Both types belong to this habitat type.

Figure 19A

Figure 19B

Figure 20. Idaho fescue/Richardson's needlegrass habitat type

The map shows areas of the Idaho fescue/Richardson's needlegrass type, a mesic grassland intermixed with Douglas-fir stands (Fig. 20A). It is of limited distribution in the park but is a productive part of the winter range. The plants in Figure 20B are clumps of Richardson's needlegrass. Note the abundance of narrow leaves. When the flowering stalks are fully developed this type presents a delightful sight with the graceful, nodding inflorescences waving in the breeze.

Figure 20A

Figure 20B

Figure 21. Big sagebrush/bluebunch wheatgrass habitat type

The big sagebrush/bluebunch wheatgrass type is found only at the warmer lower elevations (shown in the map) near the North Entrance. It is the driest shrub-dominated vegetation in the park. Bluebunch wheatgrass is shown in Figure 21B. Figure 21A shows the short stature of the sagebrush typical of this dry type.

Elk and antelope browsing have kept most of the big sagebrush on these sites small and hedged, but given protection from native browsers or a little added snow moisture the sagebrush can become dominant. This type is not very productive but does provide winter range, especially for antelope.

Figure 21A

Figure 21B

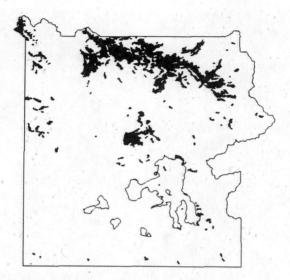

Figure 22. Big sagebrush/Idaho fescue habitat type

There are two phases of the big sagebrush/Idaho fescue type in the park. These are distributed throughout the park but are most common in the Lamar and lower Lamar River valleys, as shown in the map. They occur over a wide range of elevations and provide both winter and summer range. On the drier sites suitable for this vegetation is the Idaho fescue phase, but where the soils are more moist and deeper there is a sticky geranium phase. The dense herbaceous vegetation is seen in Figure 22B. Sticky geranium is the flower in the center. Figure 22A shows the dense large sagebrushes common on this type. Together with its related grassland type, Idaho fescue/bearded wheatgrass, big sagebrush/Idaho fescue accounts for slightly more than half of all the nonforested vegetation. These two types are probably most responsible for the large number of grazers that inhabit the park.

Figure 22A

Figure 22B

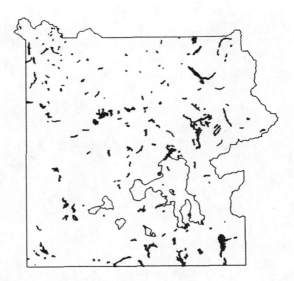

Figure 23. Tufted hairgrass/sedge habitat type

Tufted hairgrass/sedge type grows in swales and grassland sites that receive a lot of additional water. These sites are scattered throughout the park in the areas shown in the map. At lower elevations these plant communities are an important part of the winter range, producing most of the forage eaten by the animals. In those sites that are too wet for Idaho fescue but still dry enough for tufted hairgrass the aquatic and semi-aquatic sedges become more abundant and form the tufted hairgrass/sedge types. These sites dry out early enough not to be marshes. Sites that are slightly drier support an Idaho fescue/tufted hairgrass habitat type. Figure 23B shows the clumped nature of tufted hairgrass, from which the name is derived. Figure 23A shows a swale in the northern part of the park.

Figure 23A

Figure 23B

Figure 24. Silver sage/Idaho fescue habitat type

The silver sage/Idaho fescue type is scattered throughout the park along stream banks and springs and in seep areas such as the Hayden and Pelican valleys, as shown in the map. This type grows where the soil is too wet for big sagebrush roots to survive. Figure 24A shows the shrubby aspect of the community. The silver sage is two to three feet tall. The long smooth leaves of the silver sage can be seen in Figure 24B. The area in Figures 24A and 24B burned during the 1988 fires, but some of the silver sage resprouted from the roots and the grass clumps were unharmed. The area will soon look like it does in Figures 24A and 24B. In the northern part of the park, shrubby cinquefoil is mixed with the species of this type to form perhaps another habitat type or at least a phase of either a shrubby cinquefoil habitat type or a silver sage type.

Figure 24A

Figure 24B

Figure 25. Sedge marshes and other very wet areas

Sedge marshes and other very wet areas occur in the areas shown in the map wherever groundwater and topography combine to produce standing water throughout the growing season. Large expanses of this type are seen in the Bechler meadows in the southwest corner of the park. They are dominated by various species of sedges such as water sedge or inflated sedge. Around the fringes of this type, tufted hairgrass/sedge habitat type (see Fig. 23) and the wet forest (see Fig. 16) usually occur. Where these types occur on winter ranges they provide abundant winter forage for the elk and bison, who dig down through the snow to get at the dead sedge leaves. The sedge leaves, shown in Figure 25B, are 18 inches to 2 feet long and up to one-half inch wide. The generally flat nature of these marshes is shown in Figure 25A. These sedges will sometimes form a dense mat that floats on pond or lake surfaces near the shore.

Figure 25A

Figure 25B

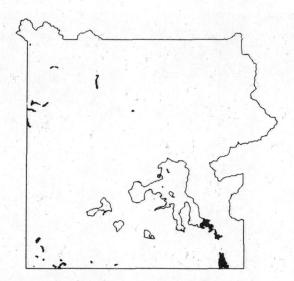

Figure 26. Willow/sedge habitat types

Willow types are distributed along the streams (shown in Fig. 26A) and near many seeps throughout the park. The largest concentration is on the delta of the Yellowstone River where it enters Yellowstone Lake (shown in the map). Large areas of willows also occur in the Gallatin and Madison river valleys and along several small creeks throughout the park. Smaller stands are associated with seep areas.

Willow/sedge types are a very heterogeneous group of wet types dominated by various species of willows. Sedges and reedgrasses are usually found under the willows, as seen in Figure 26B. The various species of willow seem to occupy different habitat types, although there is some degree of overlap. Few species are common to most willow stands, but moist area forbs such as graceful cinquefoil, meadow pussytoes, and western mountain aster are commonly encountered.

In areas of ungulate winter range, the willows are severely browsed and hedged. Some observers maintain that this is a sign of overgrazing and therefore too many ungulates are present. Transects installed with range exclosures that were constructed 25 to 30 years ago do not indicate that this severe browsing is sufficient to kill the willow plants. In the few sites suitable for establishment of these willow species, willows have established in the face of the severe browsing. It appears that willows have evolved some mechanism for surviving severe browsing.

Figure 26A

Figure 26B

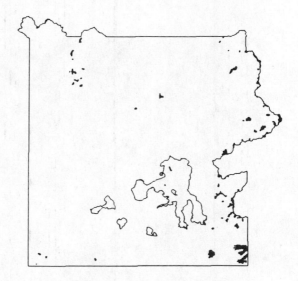

Figure 27. Alpine tundra

The alpine tundra group of types occurs mainly above 10,000 feet in the Washburn, Absaroka, and Gallatin ranges (shown in the map). Other parts of the park are not high enough to support these types.

The alpine tundra group is a diverse group of habitat types. Some types are dominated by a thick turf of alpine grasses and forbs; some are dry and rocky with a more open aspect, as that shown in Figure 27A; and some appear to be a grass turf but are mixed with dwarf willows such as snow willow, arctic willow, and cascade willow. Common grass species are sheep fescue, timberland bluegrass, Sandberg's bluegrass, Cusick's bluegrass, and the grass-like spiked woodrush. Common forbs include silvery lupine, arctic sandwort, and lanceleaf stonecrop. As shown in Figure 27B, the plants are small and close to the ground, where they are protected from the winds and are kept warm by the bright sunlight absorbed by the soil, rocks, and other plants.

Figure 27A

Figure 27B

TABLE 4

Characteristics of shrub and grass habitat types (indicator species and dominant species are in capital letters)

Phase	Distribution*	Altitude (feet)	Common species	Soil condition
Bluebunch wheatgrass/Sandberg's bluegrass habitat type needle-and-thread phase	Occurs only at the park's lowest elevations on alluvial flats of the Yellowstone River; occupies less than 1% of park	5,200–5,400	A grassland dominated by NEEDLE-AND-THREAD, BLUE-BUNCH WHEATGRASS, JUNEGRASS, and SANDBERG'S BLUEGRASS; FRINGED SAGE, common rabbitbrush	Derived from silty, coarse gravels
Idaho fescue/bluebunch wheatgrass habitat type	Occurs throughout the Yellowstone-Lamar River Valleys on south-facing slopes where sagebrush cannot grow; occupies 1% of park	5,500–6,500	A grassland: IDAHO FESCUE, BLUE-BUNCH WHEAT-GRASS, junegrass, Sandberg's bluegrass, western needlegrass, yarrow, rosy pussytoes, ballhead sandwort, common rabbitbrush, big sagebrush	Derived from andesite and sedimentary tills; good fertility; dry

Idaho fescue/bearded wheatgrass habitat type bearded wheatgrass phase	Most common in the Gallatin and Absaroka ranges; occupies 2% of the nonforested sites	7,500–10,000	A mesic forb-grassland of the subalpine zone dominated by IDAHO FESCUE: BEARDED WHEATGRASS always present; western needlegrass, timber oatgrass, junegrass; forbs are conspicuous, including prairie smoke, yarrow, mountain dandelion	Good mineral nutrition but on the dry side; derived from the andesitic volcanics
sticky geranium phase	Moister than phase described above but with same general distribution; occupies 22% of nonforested sites		Pocket-gopher activity is often quite high; occasionally, places where Idaho fescue is nearly absent and taller forbs are common, including western stickseed, yampa, giant frasera, and goldenrod; STICKY GERANIUM, GRACEFUL CINQUEFOIL, California brome, timber oatgrass, Raynold's sedge	Good mineral and moisture conditions; usually deep; derived from andesitic volcanics

TABLE 4
(continued)

Phase	Distribution*	Altitude (feet)	Common species	Soil condition
Idaho fescue/tufted hairgrass habitat type	A high-elevation grass-land most common in southwest corner; occu-pies 3% of nonforested sites	8,500–10,000	IDAHO FESCUE, TUFTED HAIR-GRASS, alpine timothy, spiked woodrush, sedges, numerous forbs, Ameri-can bistort, clover, silvery lupine, yarrow, diverse-leaved cinquefoil	Derived from alluvial material; usually wet and cold; supplemental moisture available but no standing water in summer
Idaho fescue/Richardson's needlegrass habitat type	Limited occurrence in the park; found on fairly flat terraces in the upper portion of the Yellowstone-Lamar River Valleys; occupies less	6,300–6,700	A grassland dominated by IDAHO FESCUE with a good represen-tation of RICHARD-SON'S NEEDLEGRASS; western needlegrass and	Derived from glacial till from Absaroka volcanics, sedimentary rocks, and rhyolite

89

Habitat type	Description	Elevation	Vegetation	Soil
	...than 1% of the nonforested sites		sticky geranium always present; yarrow, graceful cinquefoil, and hairy golden-aster are common	
Tufted hairgrass/sedge habitat type	A grassland type; commonly found in drainages where silts and organic matter have accumulated; distributed almost throughout the park above 6,000 ft. wherever sufficient groundwater accumulates; occupies 14% of nonforested sites	+6,000	TUFTED HAIRGRASS, SEDGES such as BLACK-AND-WHITE-SCALED SEDGE, SLENDER BEAKED SEDGE; American bistort, meadow pussytoes, graceful cinquefoil	Derived from alluvial material; high in clay, silt, and organic matter poorly drained
Big sagebrush/bluebunch wheatgrass habitat type	Occurs only at the lowest elevations of the park in the lower Yellowstone-Lamar River Valleys; occupies less than 1% of nonforested sites		A dry shrubland of BIG SAGEBRUSH interspersed with BLUEBUNCH WHEATGRASS; junegrass, Sandberg's bluegrass, needle-and-thread grass	Derived from largely andesitic rocks and glacial kame (sand and gravel deposited by rivers running on glaciers) material of andesitic origin

TABLE 4
(continued)

Phase	Distribution*	Altitude (feet)	Common species	Soil condition
Big sagebrush/Idaho fescue habitat type	Most common in the Yellowstone-Lamar River Valleys, where it covers most of terrain above 6,800; occurs in other parts of park where sagebrush occurs, such as Hayden Valley and the Gallatin Range; occupies 8% of non-forested sites	6,800–9,500	A moist shrubland of BIG SAGEBRUSH interspersed with IDAHO FESCUE; junegrass and occasionally bluebunch wheatgrass occur with Idaho fescue; common rabbitbrush, fringed sagebrush, prairie smoke	Derived from andesitic rocks or materials derived from them
sticky geranium phase	Occurs on the middle to upper elevations of the Yellowstone-Lamar River Valleys in the northern portion of the park; also well repre-	6,800–9,500	A moist phase of the habitat type described above; has a greater standing crop of grasses and forbs; timber oatgrass, California brome,	Moist, deep soil with good fertility, medium texture

Habitat type	Distribution	Elevation; dominant species	Soil
	sented in the Gallatin Range and both Hayden and Pelican valleys; occupies 20% of non-forested sites	bearded wheatgrass, Raynold's sedge, sticky geranium, Rocky Mountain helianthella, graceful cinquefoil, sulfur buckwheat	
Silver sage/Idaho fescue habitat type	A wet-area type distributed along most of the middle to upper elevation water courses; greatest concentrations found in Pelican and Hayden valleys and Swan Lake Flat; associated with areas of high water table such as stream banks, seeps, or areas of perched water tables in old lake sediments; occupies 4% of nonforested sites	7,000–8,000 SILVER SAGE, IDAHO FESCUE, tufted hairgrass, sedge species, shrubby cinquefoil	Seasonally saturated, fine to medium texture

TABLE 4
(continued)

Phase	Distribution*	Altitude (feet)	Common species	Soil condition
Willow/sedge habitat types	Distributed along streams and near many seeps throughout the park; largest concentration on delta of the Yellowstone River where it enters Yellowstone Lake; large areas also occur on Gallatin and Madison rivers and several small creeks throughout the park; smaller stands are associated with seep areas throughout the park; occupies 3% of non-forested sites	6,000–9,000	A very heterogeneous group of wet types dominated by various species of willow; various species of willow seem to occupy different habitat types, some overlap occurs. Common species include sedges, reedgrasses, graceful cinquefoil, meadow pussytoes, western mountain aster, but few species are common to most stands	Wet to saturated, coarse texture
Sedge marshes	A diverse group of habitat types occurring throughout the park on	6,000–9,000	Wet site sedges such as water, inflated, and Nebraska sedges	Soils are saturated usually with acidic water

	sites that are saturated for most of the growing season, conditions unsuitable for shrubby species			
Alpine tundra habitat type	A diverse group of habitat types occurring mainly above 10,000 ft. in the Washburn, Absaroka, and Gallatin ranges (other areas are not high enough); occupies 4% of nonforested sites	+10,000	Some types dominated by a thick turf of alpine grasses and forbs; some are dry and rocky with a more open aspect; some appear to be a grass turf but are mixed with dwarf willows such as snow willow, arctic willow, and Cascade willow. Common species: sheep fescue, timberline bluegrass, Sandberg's bluegrass, Cusick's bluegrass, spiked woodrush, silvery lupine, arctic sandwort, lanceleaf stonecrop	Very cold soils, including some permafrost, usually good mineral and moisture status

*The park can be divided into five geovegetation provinces: Gallatin Range, Absaroka Range, Central Plateaus, Southwest Plateaus, and Yellowstone-Lamar River Valleys. Descriptions of these provinces are in Chapter 6.

In areas of ungulate winter range, the willows are severely browsed and hedged. Some observers maintain that this is a sign of overgrazing and therefore too many ungulates are present. Transects installed with range exclosures that were constructed 25 to 30 years ago do not indicate that this severe browsing is sufficient to kill the willow plants. In the few sites suitable for these species, willows have established in the face of the severe browsing. It appears, therefore, that willows have evolved some mechanism for surviving severe browsing.

Alpine tundra. The alpine tundra group is a diverse group of habitat types that occurs mainly above the 10,000-foot elevation in the Washburn, Absaroka, and Gallatin mountain ranges. Other parts of the park are not at a high enough elevation to support these types. Some types are dominated by a thick turf of alpine grasses and forbs; some are dry and rocky with the plants distributed in isolated clumps; and some appear to be a grass turf but are mixed with dwarf willows such as snow willow, arctic willow, and Cascade willow. Common grass species are sheep fescue, timberland bluegrass, Sandberg's bluegrass, Cusick's bluegrass, and the grasslike spiked woodrush. Common forbs include silvery lupine, arctic sandwort, and lanceleaf stonecrop.

Aspen Stands

Aspen is not a major forest species in Yellowstone. It occurs throughout the park in various contexts but seldom in extensive stands of more than ten acres. Yellowstone is apparently on the edge of good aspen habitat. For these reasons, descriptions of the various aspen communities are not included here. However, aspen is a fascinating species, so some of its peculiarities are discussed in the next few paragraphs.

An aspen seed is very small and can be carried long distances on the small puff of cotton to which it is attached. There are enough seeds produced and they are distributed widely enough that some seeds should be deposited in any available germination sites. However, the small size of the seed does not allow for much food storage to help the germling compete with any other vegetation on the site or to allow it to withstand dry periods after it germinates. The seedlings have a high moisture requirement and die if they become even moderately dry. They also must have a lot of sun to permit the photosynthetic machinery to produce more food than is used by the plant for growth and the processes of living. Fortunately, the seedlings do not need a well-developed soil with lots of organic matter.

These exacting requirements are rarely found in a landscape where soil has had long to develop. Moist sites have a dense mantle of vegetation, and very few disturbances are severe enough to destroy that vegetation. Sites suitable for aspen seedling establishment do occur on landslides, earthquake scarps, gravel bars in rivers, and the rubble of retreating glaciers. Occasionally, with the right weather conditions, numerous sites may be found in burned forests and burned sedge marshes.

Seeds do occasionally find a suitable site and become established. As the seedling grows into a small tree, it develops an extensive lateral root system just below the soil surface. In time, the tree begins to put up root sprouts along its lateral root system, producing an interconnected group of stems that are genetically identical to each other. These groups of identical trees are referred to as clones. Over time, some of the interconnections may break down, but each tree in a clone remains connected to several other trees.

The clone expands until it meets another aspen clone or fills all the suitable habitat. The lateral roots may even extend into marginal habitat and produce root suckers supported by their connection to the roots of stems in favorable habitat. If these stems are not browsed off, a fringe of stunted trees develops on the margin of the clone.

Clones can be distinguished from one another by various morphological and behavioral differences. Some clones have slightly whiter bark. Others have a different branching pattern. The clones are easiest to distinguish in the spring or fall. Some clones begin to leaf out before others and stand out from their neighbors in the spring. Other clones begin to turn yellow in the fall before their neighbors. In areas where the climate is highly suitable for aspen, such as Utah and Colorado, it is common to see scattered groups of aspen turning yellow throughout a stand that covers a

Figure 28. An aspen stand in Lamar Valley

hillside. Each of these groups is a different clone started from different seeds. From the size of some of these clones, some authors have speculated that the seed that produced the clone may have germinated as much as a few million years ago (3).

In Yellowstone, it is not unreasonable to assume that many of the clones present today started as the glaciers retreated, 12,000 to 14,000 years ago. If this is the case, the aspen we see now have lived through a lot of climatic and environmental changes. It is conceivable that the aspen clones being browsed by deer and elk today were once fed upon on by mammoth, horses, and camels.

Aspen have a characteristic ability to survive destruction of their aboveground parts. Following a fire, for example, the clone simply sends up a very dense stand of root sprouts from its extensive underground root system. Densities of more than 200,000 stems per acre have been recorded. If food reserves in the roots are sufficient these sprouts can grow as much as six to eight feet the first year. The faster growing sprouts begin to suppress their shorter companions, and over time the stand thins out.

The root sprouts that come up after a fire are different from those produced later. They have higher growth rates with longer distance between leaves. These stems produce few, if any, branches, and those that do grow are usually dropped in the fall with the leaves, concentrating growth in the central stem. The leaves are much larger (up to six inches wide) and both leaves and stems have a higher concentration of chemicals that are toxic to insects and other animals. This phenomenon is very common in woody plants and is called juvenility because of the consequent inability to produce flowers. After two or three years, the stems switch from the juvenile form to the adult form. They begin to retain their branches, growth rates slow down, and the leaves do not grow as large. Just what causes this switch from juvenile to adult growth or vice versa has not been investigated in aspen. It is possible that the switch to juvenility is caused by fire.

Another phenomenon that aspen share with other plants is the production of growth regulators called auxins. Auxins are produced in the buds and actively growing leaves and are transported down the stem. The concentration of auxins therefore increases downward. These chemicals retard growth and suppress the growth of buds and root sprouts. This regulation helps aspen in two ways: It limits the majority of leaf growth to the ends of the branches, where the sun is brightest, and retards the initiation of root suckers. Root suckers trying to grow in the shade of larger stems would not have enough sunlight to produce all the food needed for growth; those on the edge of the stand would be in marginal habitat and thus would be less likely to contribute to the food reserves in the roots. Root suckers in either situation would be a drain on energy reserves, which are better used to produce branches on the tops of the trees, where the most food can be produced.

This regulation is not perfect. Most older, unbrowsed aspen stands have smaller stems under their canopy and on their fringes. A few suckers can arise when a late spring frost kills the actively growing buds or a root segment is severed from the rest of the roots. These suckers are usually in the adult rather than the juvenile condition, and their number per acre is not nearly as high as that following a fire.

One of the esthetic characteristics of aspen is the almost stark white bark with sharply contrasting black patterns. These black patterns are scars from earlier events. The scar produced when a leaf falls from a small stem grows to several inches in width as the stem increases in size. Frost cracks and toothmarks from animals also increase in size as the bark grows to cover the increasing girth of the trunk. Even initials carved on the trunk continue to grow as the tree gets older. In some isolated areas of southern Wyoming where aspen trees grow well, it is said that some of the trunks sport artwork (produced by lonely sheep herders) that has grown noticeably larger over the years.

All these interesting and seemingly unconnected characteristics are important in understanding aspen and its relationship to other organisms, especially browsing animals. Some range management and wildlife management professionals who have visited the winter range in northern Yellowstone have expressed concern about the future of aspen there. Their concern is based on several observations about the condition of the aspen stands. Small trees, which they feel are needed to replace the older trees when they die, are lacking or are heavily browsed by the high populations of elk and other animals. The lower six to seven feet of the trunks of all the trees are scarred by animal feeding, and many of the trunks are host to a wide variety of fungal diseases. When an aspen tree falls over in the winter the bark is quickly eaten off, right down to the lower six to seven feet where the scar tissue begins.

To determine the effects of browsing on aspen, fences were placed around some aspen clones in the late 1950s and early 1960s. There are now trees in the exclosure, 20 to 30 feet tall, that appear to be available to replace the older trees when they die. One fortuitous experiment was conducted when aspen shoots grew up inside an abandoned haypen that had been constructed in the 1920s. In 1936, this small stand was split in two by a wire fence and was designated Aspen Plot No. 25. The fate of the stems was followed over the next several years. All the large stems outside the fence were quickly girdled by the elk and are now gone. Those inside the exclosure are now good-sized trees. These observations show that aspen is very tasty to elk and other browsers.

It would appear that aspen may eventually be lost from the winter range in the park, given the numbers of these animals that now use the range. However, those who would predict the loss of aspen from the Yellowstone ecosystem must explain the aspen that now exist on the winter range. Three hypotheses are most commonly given: 1) Browsers (elk) are relatively new to the area, and the trees grew up before they arrived (4); 2) for some reason, elk numbers periodically dropped low enough and stayed low long enough for the aspen to grow above the reach of elk and maintain themselves on the site (5); and 3) past fires were large enough to allow the production of so many aspen shoots that the elk could not eat them all, so some survived to become trees (1). Climate may also have somehow differed in the past and helped aspen to cope with browsing.

But before we mourn the loss of aspen in Yellowstone, let's examine each of the observations in light of what we know about aspen along with some additional observations. One must be very careful when trying to understand aspen ecology. Even the seemingly simple process of reproduction must be carefully interpreted. The small trees under the canopy of an aspen clone are not new individuals, as they are in a nonclonal species such as lodgepole pine. Instead, they are just smaller branches arising from the roots of an established larger organism.

Aspen stems that grew up inside the exclosure have branches from the ground up. Most of the larger trees across the winter range have no branches and no branch scars below six to seven feet. In an aspen stand ten miles north of the park that was burned to improve browse for wildlife, the aspen resprouted vigorously but were completely browsed off during the first winter. However, the next winter the stand was only lightly browsed, and by the fourth growing season it had grown above the browsing line. One short unpublished study looked at the pith traces in the center of the lower part of ten tree trunks in five stands across the elk range and determined that all the trees had been browsed once or twice when they were little. Inspection of areas where aspen clones appear to have disappeared in the past reveals the current presence of aspen. The plants are just very small and appear to resprout every year. A closer look at Aspen Plot No. 25 reveals that aspen are still present outside the fence. In fact, the whole meadow appears to have small aspen sprouts.

The most logical explanation for the events that transpired at Aspen Plot No. 25 would be the following. When the haypen fence was put up, it enclosed and protected a group of small, inconspicuous aspen sprouts in a meadow full of such sprouts. When the haypen was abandoned, these shoots were able to grow taller, and when the pole fence was torn down and the wire fence was put up around half of the group, those stems on the outside simply reverted to their earlier form. If this is the case, then aspen are able to live longer than 50 years in a form that is similar to perennial herbs. Comparison of old photographs with current conditions is bringing to light other instances of this ability to persist for long periods after the "trees" are gone.

All of this suggests the following alternative explanation for the presence of today's aspen stands. When conditions are optimal for aspen they store large amounts of food in the root system. If fire kills all the aboveground stems on the clone, there is enough strength in the roots to push the suckers above the browsing level. The switch to juvenility and the production of toxins in the stem tissue discourages the girdling of the stems, and the experimental nibbling by the animals causes scars that grow with the tree and protect it throughout its life. In suboptimal conditions, aspen remain in a hedged shrub form or, in marginal conditions, even in a perennial herb form.

However, this hypothesis does not explain one observation: All existing aspen stands were browsed off once or twice, including the ones from the range-improvement burn north of the park. It could be that toxin production is quite variable from year to year depending on climate or that the stems must be browsed once to induce the plant to produce the toxins. This would explain the heavy browsing after the first year and the light browsing after the second year. Research is presently being conducted to demonstrate whether this alternative hypothesis is true.

The proper interpretation of aspen ecology is important in deciding the best management strategy. Some have suggested fencing aspen clones to allow the little ones to grow above browsing level and preserve the esthetic stands of large aspen trees. The fences could then be taken down and the aspen allowed to continue to grow into larger trees. Others have suggested that the elk population be periodically reduced sufficiently to allow the aspen to escape browsing. If the alternative explanation given here is true, both management techniques would fail. As soon as the fences were taken down or the elk population built up, the aspen stems would be girdled and revert to their short form because they would lack the protection gained during juvenility in the lower six to seven feet of the stem.

Thermal Communities

Wide variations of temperature are encountered in the numerous geyser basins in the park. Heat coming from the ground has an important influence on plant communities, affecting the aboveground portion of the plants as well as their roots. More than soil and air temperature are affected, as the heat also affects the water regime. Higher temperatures cause water to evaporate faster, and winter snow depth is influenced by the thermal output of the ground. It is common in the winter to see two to three feet of snow perched atop logs, which provide insulation from the bare warm ground below.

It is reasonable to expect tropical conditions to occur in these thermal areas. Indeed, there are two tropical species that appear out of place in Yellowstone, both associated with thermally heated water. One, *Chara xeylanica* (so far no one has given it a common name), is a primitive aquatic plant that fits somewhere between algae and the higher plants. The other, yellow spike-rush, belongs to a genus of vascular plants that grow equally well either in or near water.

Heat-source movement represents another important variable for these communities. Heat is carried to the surface primarily by water circulating through the ground. The dissolved minerals in the water precipitate and seal the channel periodically, forcing the water to find a new route to the surface. The frequency of this occurrence is highly variable, depending on both earthquakes and channel sizes and configurations. One study of the influence of heat on the vegetation of thermal areas described the various communities found at different temperatures (1). The study showed that the group of plants growing on the site indicated the tem-

Figure 29A

Figure 29B

Figure 29. Vegetation on thermally influenced soil in Lower Geyser Basin

Figure 29A shows a large flat near Fountain Paint Pots covered by a very short grassland. The size of the grass clumps can be seen in Figure 29B by comparison with the pocket-gopher tunnel castings, which are about 3 to 4 inches in diameter. Several species of grasses are salt tolerant.

perature of the ground. Table 5 lists the species common to different temperature levels.

The plants of the hottest areas are all very short. Even in winter, the air near the ground is heated to temperatures that are adequate for plant growth. However, when the wind blows, the air temperature just two inches above the ground can drop from 72°F to –40°F instantaneously. Some plants, such as yellow monkeyflowers, have both a flat winter form, to take advantage of the pocket of warm air near the ground, and an upright summer form. Corrugate-seeded spurge is known to flower in January in the thermal areas; this diminutive flowering plant grows flat on the ground. Other species flower as much as a month earlier on the warmer ground than plants of the same species on the ground just beyond the thermal area's influence.

Water flowing from the thermal features contains many dissolved substances. Plant communities that depend on this water for moisture show a definite influence of these dissolved salts. Seaside arrowgrass, alkali cordgrass, meadow barley, baltic rush, tufted hairgrass, and other salt-tolerant species are commonly found in these situations.

One species, Ross's bentgrass, is found only in the thermal envi-

TABLE 5

Plant species growing in different temperature zones along thermal gradients in the geyser basins

Temperature (°F)	Species
>65	Bare ground except where insulated by a humus layer. Here, moss mats provide a rooting medium for other heat-tolerant species.
50–65	Moss zone, including *Rhacomitrium canescens, Bryum pseudotriquetrum, Ceratodon purpureus, Pohlia nutans,* and *Dicranum muhlenbeckii.**
25–50	Grass zone, dominated by Nuttall's alkali-grass, thermal western witchgrass, poverty danthonia, winter bentgrass, cheatgrass, and bluegrasses.
23–37	Herb zone, occasionally mixed with the grass zone, including hairy golden-aster, sheep sorrel, fireweed, Canada thistle, and spear-leaf fleabane.

*Scientific names were used for mosses because common names are not available.

ronment. It is a small annual, germinating in the late winter and blooming before spring comes to the snowbound landscape surrounding the thermal areas. This is the only known plant species endemic to Yellowstone. So far, this species has been found only in the geyser basins near Old Faithful (Upper, Middle, and Lower geyser basins), and only in areas where steam comes to the soil surface and condenses on the soil. Seeds were taken to a greenhouse to test whether the species was truly an annual or if perhaps it was a perennial that was killed every summer by heat rising from the ground in combination with the higher air temperature. The grass was a true annual and it did very well in the greenhouse environment, going through several reproductive cycles. It even spread to neighboring containers. These observations suggest that Ross's bentgrass may be best suited to a tropical environment.

Such a relatively narrow set of requirements would seem to put some interesting restrictions on this species. The annual character means the seeds must find suitable environments every year. Yet, appropriate environments shift from time to time, requiring that the species be able to move long distances. No one knows how dispersal is accomplished, but my theory is the migrations of bison or elk. Both animals winter in the geyser basins and frequent the sites where Ross's bentgrass grows. They bed down in these areas and move from thermal area to thermal area. Their hair can carry the seed or the seed embedded in mud. In the spring, they feed on the young grass shoots. These animals appear to be the perfect carrier for an organism that must move from one thermal area to another, sometimes over long distances.

3
Cover Types

As described in the introduction, the cover type classification is a means of classifying plant communities that result from succession. After fire or other disturbance removes the forest overstory, a plant community that is best suited to the environment of that site begins to develop. Many vacant sites are available for occupation, and the plants compete with each other according to the adaptations recorded in their genetic material and the conditions of the site.

The successional process is, obviously, a continuous one. Each year the trees get a little larger and the environment changes imperceptibly. The easiest way to store and retrieve information regarding the characteristics of the forest in any stage of development is to break this continuum into manageable pieces. We do this all the time with the electromagnetic spectrum. The continuous series of light-wave frequencies of the rainbow is commonly broken into seven major colors. We may not all agree just which blue-green frequency marks the division between blue and green, but we all agree that frequencies some distance from the boundary are either blue or green. This classification makes possible a great deal of information storage, retrieval, and transfer.

We can readily determine whether a stand of trees is in an early, middle, or late stage of succession; adding the recently disturbed class and a climax class provides us with five easily recognizable classes. We might not agree on whether a stand is early-middle or late-early, but at these boundaries it may not be too significant that we agree as long as we recognize the nearness of the boundary.

The tree species that dominates a successional stage is determined by site conditions. Habitat type is a classification of site conditions, but several habitat types share successional tree species. I have chosen to use the term *cover type* over *successional stage* in order to incorporate the ideas of both dominant tree species and time since last disturbance. In the following descriptions of the cover types of Yellowstone, the classes are given a letter code designating the dominant tree species followed by a number indicating the progression of age. Thus, the name LP2 indicates a stand dominated by lodgepole pine in the middle of its successional progress, while DF0 designates a stand of very young Douglas-fir trees.

Chronological ages of the classes are only approximate and are not as important as the stand structure. To indicate how near the boundary between two stages a particular stand may be, a decimal value may be given to the number. For example, an older lodgepole pine stand may be designated LP2.9 by one person whereas someone else might call it LP3.1. Both observers, however, would agree that the stand was not LP2.5 or LP3.5.

In determining the cover type of a stand, it is useful to look at the dead trees as well as the live ones. Dead trees can tell much about stand dynamics. As the later stages are reached, the successional species will be largely represented as dead trunks on the forest floor. However, care must be taken in examining stands killed by disease or insects, as the characteristics of such stands may not easily fit the cover type description.

The different cover types encountered in Yellowstone and the ways fires behave in each of the types are described in the next several pages. Small silhouettes appear with the descriptions as a visual aid. The stage of growth of the stand is very important in determining fire behavior, largely because of the variety of ways fuels may have accumulated and become distributed.

Cover Type Descriptions

LP0: The LP0 cover type represents recently burned forests where lodgepole pine is expected to colonize the site, or has done so already, but reforestation has not yet produced a closed canopy. Within the first few years the forest floor is covered by species that, for the most part, were present before the fire or other disturbance. Many of the plants present before the disturbance simply resprout.

Ross's sedge accounts for the majority of plant cover for several years. Wild strawberries, leafy aster, and elk sedge occur commonly. These stands are approximately 0 to 40 years old.

Fuels in this cover type consist mostly of forbs, grasses, and rotten logs. Immediately after a fire, sound logs begin to rot and seeds begin to germinate. As time goes on, the number of rotten logs, tree seedlings, and saplings increases. Under normal moisture conditions, only the rotten logs burn, drying and burning some of the herbaceous growth next to them. Occasionally, small trees or clumps of small trees burn if fuel conditions at their base are just right. If the firebrand "rain" is heavy enough, most of the rotten logs will burn. Under very dry conditions (drought), the herbaceous growth may dry enough to carry a flaming front. With the right wind and moisture conditions, fire spread through this type is possible, though rare. Fire starts are moderately common in this type because of the rotten wood.

LP1: The LP1 cover type consists of very dense stands of small-diameter lodgepole pine, usually shorter than the neighboring stands. An understory of small trees is nonexistent, and forest floor vegetation is very sparse. Rotten logs from the previous forest may still be present on the forest floor. Stands are usually 50 to 150 years old.

Fuels here are essentially confined to the tree crowns of these lodgepole stands. The compact needle litter burns with flames only an inch or so high or as a smoldering fire. Under normal fire season moisture conditions, this type is nearly unburnable. Firebrands may find an occasional rotten log and burn out a small spot. Under very dry conditions with high winds, fire may spread through the canopy if a crowning fire reaches the stand. Fire spread will stop, however, if the wind ceases even momentarily. There are no fuels to get the fire back into the canopy even if the wind should return. Fire starts in this type are very rare.

LP2: LP2 cover type stands are closed-canopy stands dominated by lodgepole pine. The original overstory is still largely intact. The understory usually consists of Engelmann spruce and subalpine fir seedlings and saplings up to eight feet tall. The forest floor is typically well covered with herbaceous vegetation and grouse whortleberry. These stands are usually 150 to 300 years old.

This type can be considered transitional between the almost unburnable LP1 and the highly burnable LP3. At either extreme, the stands mapped as LP2 may have fire-behavior characteristics somewhat like stands designated a class higher or lower. However, stands halfway between the endpoints will have their own unique characteristics. Fuels in this type are largely herbaceous or low shrubs such as grouse whortleberry. Concentrations of small trees may also provide fuel.

Under normal conditions, this type is very difficult to burn, and fire starts are rare. The understory vegetation stays moist enough to retard fire spread and very few rotten logs are available. Under very dry conditions, the herbaceous growth may carry the fire. Fire spread, however, is very slow because the canopy prevents wind from reaching the flames. If a dense undergrowth of globe huckleberry develops and trees killed by bark beetles have fallen to contribute understory fuels, crowning is possible. In the older stands, sufficient young trees may be on hand to allow crowning in spots.

Bark-beetle kill is common in this cover type; however, experience with natural fires in Yellowstone has shown that beetle-killed trees affect fire behavior very little. The red crowns (needles of recently killed trees turn red as they die) are much drier than the green crowns, but crowning is still dependent on the existence of sufficient understory fuels, and red crowns comprise only a fraction of the tree crowns even in heavily infested areas. Once the needles fall off the trees, crown fuels are reduced. Beetles may even reduce the occurrence of crown fires in older stands (see the section on insects in Chapter 7).

LP3: The canopy of LP3 stands is quite ragged, consisting predominantly of lodgepole pine but containing some Engelmann spruce, subalpine fir, and whitebark pine. The understory consists of small to large spruce and fir seedlings and saplings. The forest floor has the appearance of that under climax spruce-fir stands. These stands are usually more than 300 years old.

Fuels in this type ignite easily and burn readily in only moderately dry conditions. Young trees contribute to understory fuels and fuels continuous with the overstory. Spruce and fir trees are scattered among the overstory and may add to the dead-and-down

fuels in the understory. On the better growing sites, globe huckleberry may also significantly increase the fuels. Lichen accumulations in older trees contribute to the fuel load and make the crown
burn easily; lightning strikes and firebrands find an easily burnable
substrate in these crowns. This type supports most of the spectacular fires. Even under moderately dry moisture conditions this
type burns. If winds are present, crowning and spotting are nearly inevitable. Without winds, torching occurs with local spotting.
Under dry conditions, local crowning and smoke column development is possible even without wind. Spotting is very common and
is the largest contributor to fire spread. Under wet conditions, these
stands allow fires to smolder and persist but spread is minimal.
Deep litter and duff accumulations and rotten logs protected from
precipitation by overstory trees provide sites where fires can persist for several weeks. Most fires start in this cover type.

LP: LP stands are climax stands of lodgepole pine that are
beginning to break up. The overstory is dominated by lodgepole
pine with some whitebark pine often present. Young lodgepole
pine are always present in the understory and are usually, but not
always, accompanied by whitebark pine. Stands occur mostly on
rhyolite or other dry soils and are usually more than 300 years old.
The stands do not go through an LP3 stage because spruce and
fir cannot grow on these sites.

Growing conditions are poor in this type, therefore fuels are
sparse. Lodgepole pine forms the overstory and most of the understory, and herbs and small shrubs are widely scattered. Under normal conditions, this type burns very poorly. Under dry, windy
conditions, local areas may burn and spots may develop into local
crowning where a firebrand finds the occasional concentration of
understory fuels. The result is a very spotty burn. Rapid spread
through this type is difficult, and fire starts are rare.

SF: SF stands are climax stands dominated by Engelmann
spruce and subalpine fir in both the overstory and understory.
Lodgepole pine may still be a significant component in areas that
went through an LP0–LP3 series. Whitebark pine may be a significant component at high elevations on the whitebark pine phase
of the subalpine fir/grouse whortleberry habitat type. Most SF
stands in Yellowstone occur in moist areas with supplemental

groundwater. Occasionally, on very wet or cold areas, both spruce and fir will form the first postdisturbance stand and an SF0–SF1–SF2–SF series will result. The SF3 stage would be indistinguishable from the SF stage. The SF type is not common because the successional stage just prior to this type is so burnable that few stands survive to this stage.

Fuels are often abundant in the SF type. Grasses, herbs, and shrubs are common on the forest floor, as are all age classes of spruce and fir trees, but they are usually wet. Late in the season, dead vegetation may dry out sufficiently to carry a fire. In the late fall, the physiological processes that prepare the trees for winter may bring fuel moisture down to a burnable state. Under normal moisture conditions, this type is wet enough to retard fire spread. Under very dry conditions, the supplemental water may dry up and leave a high fuel load in a dry condition, which would burn quite well.

WB0: WB0 stands are recently burned whitebark pine stands, usually near upper timberline.

Fuels of this type are like those of LP0, therefore fire behavior is similar. Herbaceous vegetation may be abundant, but it is usually too green to burn well.

WB1: The WB1 type consists of evenly aged whitebark pine stands where trees are younger and shorter than those of neighboring stands.

Fuels and fire behavior are similar to LP1 stands. These are all high-elevation stands, and only rarely do they dry out enough to burn. In the rare dry year, fire spread is retarded by this type. No fire starts have been recorded.

WB2: WB2 stands are very similar to LP2 stands and are also similar in fire behavior and general appearance. Like WB1, the coolness of high elevations and poor fuel conditions make fire very rare.

WB3: WB3 stands occupy those sites where whitebark pine are the seral trees but Engelmann spruce and subalpine fir form the climax forest. Whitebark pine shares dominance with both spruce and fir and an occasional lodgepole pine in the overstory. The understory is clearly dominated by spruce and fir and is moderately dense. These stands occur above 8,600 feet elevation on good soils with moist water relationships.

Fire will burn quite readily in this type if conditions are dry.

Fire behavior is similar to that in the LP3 cover type. Fire does not occur frequently in the higher elevations.

WB: WB stands are the climax stage in the whitebark pine cover type series where soils are dry and poor in nutrients. On better sites where spruce and fir are able to grow, these two species form the climax community. WB stands are most common above 8,600 feet elevation. They are dominated by mature whitebark pine but may contain a few Engelmann spruce, subalpine fir, or lodgepole pine.

Fuels and fire behavior are similar to either LP2 or LP3. These are high-elevation types and only dry out in very dry years. Extreme fire behavior is possible in such years, with crowning and spotting especially in stands where spruce and fir trees form a significant understory.

DF0: DF0 stands are postdisturbance stands on sites where Douglas-fir are dominant as small trees. They are usually on productive sites, and the regrowth after a fire provides suitable fuel for fire in the spring or late fall, when the grasses are dried out and the shrubs have no leaves. If ignition sources were frequent enough these stands would probably establish a Douglas-fir savanna. Young Douglas-fir are moderately tolerant of fire, and a few would survive to become trees.

DF1: DF1 are evenly aged Douglas-fir stands where trees are younger and shorter than those of neighboring stands. Their appearance is similar to that of LP1 except for the numerous small, dead branches along the tree trunks from ground level to the crown. Shrubs and herbaceous growth are usually sparse.

The fuels of this type are similar to LP1, but fire behavior could be more extreme. More dead branches on the lower tree trunks and higher lichen accumulations may contribute to the load of dead, dry fuels. Rotten logs may also be more common. This type, however, is not common in the park, and therefore is not a significant contributor to overall fire behavior.

DF2: DF2 stands are similar to LP2 stands in appearance of the overstory. However, the undergrowth is much more abundant. Pinegrass often forms a sward, and snowberry or mallow ninebark may form a significant shrub layer.

Surface fires that consume the shrubs and herbaceous growth

would be common if the type received many ignitions during times when the grass is dry and the shrubs are without their leaves. However, this is very rare because in the spring the shade slows down snowmelt and evaporation of moisture from the fuels, and the grass greens up before the stand dries out enough to burn. In the fall, by the time the leaves fall off the shrubs and the grass dries up, the lightning season is over. The crowns of Douglas-fir usually do not burn as well as spruce and fir, but with enough understory fuels and dry enough weather they could burn as well as the LP3 stands.

 DF: DF stands are dominated by Douglas-fir, often in scattered islands in a nonforest matrix. They are the climax forests of the Douglas-fir cover type series. Lodgepole pine may be a component of these stands where it was the major seral species. The DF3 type does not occur in this DF0–DF series because it is indistinguishable from DF.

The understory fuels consist mostly of pinegrass with a variety of other herbs. Snowberry or mallow ninebark may contribute significantly in the shrub layer. The bark and needles of the trees do not burn as readily as those of other species; therefore, fire spread in those fuels is slower. Under normal to dry conditions, the fire may just burn off the fuels on the forest floor and leave the trees unburned. Where a dense understory of young trees has developed, crowning is possible.

PART TWO
Origin and Distribution of the Vegetation

4

Paleovegetation and Paleogeography

Vegetation covering the Yellowstone area has always been a function of worldwide climate and of modifications of that climate produced by local and regional topography. Mountains have been an aspect of the landscape since the Laramide orogeny (mountain-building episode) produced the ancestors of many of today's Rocky Mountain ranges approximately 80 million years ago.

Present vegetation is the result of past climatic forces. The rich semitropical to temperate floras that once flourished on the slopes of the mountains have been reduced and modified by the intervening climatic and topographic changes.

The well-known fossil forests of Yellowstone, together with a number of fossil localities in the general region around Yellowstone, make possible a fairly complete reconstruction of the paleovegetation of the Yellowstone region. This chapter draws heavily upon two papers: one on the paleofloras (1) and one on the tectonic and topographic aspects (2). The following discussion may be easier to follow by referring to Figure 30.

The area that is now Yellowstone has been a terrestrial environment for the last 90 million years, since the latter part of the Cretaceous Era. At that time, the climate was humid and tropical.

In the intervening time, two major worldwide events occurred that had profound effects on the vegetation that grew in this area. The first event, about 65 million years ago, was so cataclysmic that the biotic world was forever drastically changed. Recent evidence points to a meteorite impact that had enough force to put dust, smoke, and debris into the air, blocking the sun long enough to create a protracted cold period (3). Following that event, mammals became the dominant animals and reptiles became a less ob-

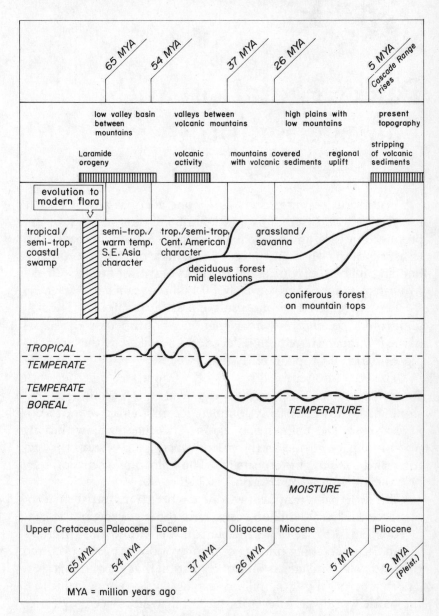

Figure 30. Vegetation, general topography, and major geologic events affecting the Yellowstone National Park area since it emerged from the Cretaceous seas

vious part of the world fauna. The world's vegetation appears to have been nearly devastated. There followed a period of widespread fern cover; these ferns probably formed pioneering communities on the devastated land. Species surviving in refugia spread into suitable habitats, establishing a new vegetation (4). Angiosperms (plants with seeds enclosed in a fruit) that had evolved earlier went through a rapid evolution to essentially modern forms.

The second event occurred about 34 million years ago, bringing an end to the Eocene (5). The mean annual temperature dropped about 20°F, and mean annual range of temperature increased from 5–10 degrees Fahrenheit to 35–50 degrees Fahrenheit. One hypothesis is that the earth encountered a cosmic cloud that left a layer of small meteorites on the ocean floor and a Saturn-type ring around the earth that shaded the winter hemisphere (the Northern Hemisphere from November to February and the Southern Hemisphere from May to August) (6). There are also other, less exotic theories.

Following that event, climate had a distinctly modern aspect. Since then, in the middle latitudes the mean annual temperature has remained fairly constant, but the winters have become warmer while the summers have cooled, thus decreasing the mean annual range of temperature.

With this time and event framework in mind, let's look at the topography and vegetation in the area that became Yellowstone National Park. Prior to the Laramide orogeny, the Yellowstone region began to rise out of the great continental seas and coastal swamps that previously covered the area. Erosion probably kept up with uplift, creating a low-lying area near sea level. Topography was flat to low, rolling hills. Ocean occupied what is now eastern Wyoming. Climate was apparently quite warm and humid since a large percentage of fossil leaves have smooth rather than toothed or lobed margins, and there are many fossils of early palms, figs, and a relative of the modern avocado, cinnamon, and sassafras. The forests were dominated by early relatives of many modern seed plants (Table 6) currently living in tropical to subtropical parts of the world (7).

During the Laramide orogeny (late Cretaceous through Paleo-

TABLE 6
Dominant species in the Late Cretaceous flora in eastern Wyoming

Fossil	Possible modern correlations	
Araucarites longifolia	*Araucarites*	screw pine
Platanophyllum montanum	Platanaceae	sycamore
Salix lancensis	*Salix*	willow
Sequoia dakotensis	*Sequoia*	redwood
Vitis stantoni	*Vitis*	grape
Dryophyllum subfalcatum	*Quercus*	oak
Fraxinus leii	*Fraxinus*	ash
Viburnum marginatum	*Viburnum*	viburnum
Cornophyllum wardii	*Cornus*	dogwood
Pistia corrugata	*Pistia*	an aquatic
Ficus	*Ficus*	figs
Sabalites	Sabalaceae	palms
Laurophyllum	Lauraceae	avocado, cinnamon, sassafras
Pistacia eriensis	*Pistacia*	pistachio nuts
Grewiopsis saportana	*Grewiopsis*	basswood

cene), large mountain masses arose around the Yellowstone area: the Beartooth uplift in the northeast corner of the present park area extended farther north and east, the Targhee uplift to the southwest, and the ancestral Gallatin Range to the northwest. Another mountain range probably extended to the northwest from the center of the present southern park boundary. It either connected with the Gallatin Range or dropped back to the basal plain somewhere in the present caldera.

The park area itself was probably a series of basins near sea level nestled between the mountain ranges (8). Vegetation was likely quite similar to the pre-Laramide vegetation in the basins, but the mountains would have had a more cold-adapted flora. The Pacific Ocean coast was near the present Oregon-Idaho border at that time (9), and no other mountain ranges intervened between the coast and the mountains around the Yellowstone area. This provided the park area a more maritime climate than currently exists.

Shortly after the orogeny subsided and things began to stabilize, volcanic activity began. This activity was predominately along two northwest-southeast tending lines that ran through the center and

TABLE 7
Elevational distribution of middle Eocene flora

Lower	Middle	Upper
figs	yew	larch
avocado	redwood	fir
palms	bald cypress	spruce
screw pine	hickory	pines
red mangrove	mulberry	hemlock
white mangrove	oak	alder
balsa	elms	cedar
myrtle	chestnut	cottonwood
breadfruit	hazelnut	willow
	holly	
	bayberry	
	wingnut	
	dogwood	
	walnut	

eastern edges of the park. Topography became predominately high volcanic mountains and narrow, near-sea-level valleys. Tree species evolved to modern forms but the climate was still warm and humid.

This area was in a broad ecotone between the cooler temperate flora to the north and the warmer, more tropical flora to the south. The plant species must have been distributed along the elevational gradient up the mountains much as they are today (see Table 7). Tropical to semitropical jungle containing breadfruit, mangroves, and other tropical species probably occurred in the valley bottoms. These species gradually relinquished dominance to broadleaved evergreen and deciduous forests consisting of elms, oaks, and maples on the middle elevations; these species, in turn, gave way to coniferous forests near the mountaintops (10). The ancestors of today's spruce and fir were there along with early lodgepole pine.

The flora during the early part of this period bore a strong resemblance to the vegetation currently found in Southeast Asia (1). By early mid-Eocene, the climate cooled and developed a summer dry period. The flora lost most of its Southeast Asian character and became like that now in Central America and southern Mexico.

Following a warm period when the region's climate reached

its most tropical state, the climate began again to cool, warmed slightly once more, then cooled gradually until the rapid cooling of the terminal Eocene event. During this period (middle Eocene), the Targhee uplift sank into the Snake River downwarp, no longer providing alluvial debris to the areas south of the park and reducing the rain shadow over the park area.

Volcanic activity continued until, during Oligocene time, the basins were filled with volcanic debris and only the upper 1,000 to 4,000 feet of the mountains, both volcanic and nonvolcanic, extended above the fill (2). The landscape looked like a large, flat plain with small volcanic mountains and little granite knobs poking through. On this higher plain (perhaps as much as 5,000 feet above sea level), climate became cooler and drier still following the terminal Eocene event.

There are no known fossil plant records from the Oligocene period in Yellowstone Park, but some generalizations can be made. Much research on modern floras has shown a relationship between temperature and forest types (11). This together with fossil floras from neighboring localities (1, 12) can be used as a guide for a plausible reconstruction.

The cool, temperate flora became more dominant. The upper slopes of the mountains were covered with coniferous forests. Deciduous hardwood forests, very similar to those now found in the eastern United States, covered the lower slopes of the mountains. These forests contained maple, oak, hickory, and walnut, as well as other familiar hardwood species. Riparian zones along the rivers and streams were dominated by deciduous hardwood forests as well. Between these riparian areas were probably large, open grasslands containing scattered trees. Fossils of a small Oligocene fauna from just south of the park boundary indicates the probability of these vegetation types (13).

These same conditions persisted through the first half of the Miocene Era. Cooling of the climate and regional uplift during the late Miocene and early Pliocene combined to create conditions in which coniferous forests expanded greatly. By 9 million years ago, hardwood deciduous trees were confined to the valley bottoms, which they shared with conifers (14). Regional uplift resulted in the reexcavation of the basins; topography became much like it is today. The Cascade Range to the west arose and blocked much of the atmospheric moisture coming from the Pacific Ocean, which was then near its present location. By the end of the Pliocene, the climate and vegetation were very similar to those of today.

The Pleistocene (or Ice Age) in the Yellowstone area was a time of cycles. Coniferous forest became tundra, then ice caps covered the area only to be replaced again by tundra and coniferous forest (15). Ice caps covered the Yellowstone area 10 to 12 times. One interglacial climate went through a distinct warming trend that allowed species now found at altitudes 1,500 to 3,000 feet lower to occupy middle elevation areas in the park (16). A vegetation developed similar to that now found on the southeast flanks of the Bighorn Mountains, about 100 miles east of the park. The major plant cover was a ponderosa pine/Douglas-fir/limber pine forest with large areas of sagebrush and grass.

During this time, the Yellowstone caldera erupted and two-thirds of at least one volcanic mountain and a large part of the Basin Creek uplift collapsed into the caldera, leaving remnants of the mountains that are now Mount Washburn and Mount Sheridan. The rhyolitic flows that followed the explosion and collapse formed the present topography of high broad plateaus with deeply incised canyons next to the steep-sided valleys of the much eroded earlier volcanic mountains. The vegetation was eliminated and had to reinvade from neighboring mountains and basins.

Following the last glacial episode, tundra was replaced by subalpine forests much like the forests of today, with Engelmann spruce, subalpine fir, and whitebark pine predominating. Lodgepole pine was also quite plentiful. About 6,000 to 7,000 years ago, climate apparently warmed, and lodgepole pine increased in importance in the vegetation (17). This increase probably resulted from a greater incidence of forest fires and from an enlarged area of habitat best suited to lodgepole pine. Since that time, climate has cooled to its present level and vegetation has assumed its present aspect. Spruce and fir have increased in importance, and treeline has descended farther down the peaks.

Climatic fluctuations are still very much a part of the vegetation. About 300 years ago, a minor cooling event known as the Little Ice Age began, undoubtedly causing some minor adjustments in Yellowstone's forests. When the Little Ice Age ended about 100 years ago, the vegetation began a readjustment that continues today. Most of the forests that burned in the 1988 fires were more than 100 years old, and as they are replaced the new trees will become established under the current climatic restraints. The new forests may not be exactly like those that burned.

A climatic reconstruction of the past 220 years based on the tree-ring record (18) shows several ups and downs in both temperature and precipitation. As climatic conditions become more or less suited to the establishment and growth requirements of different species present today, these species expand and contract their ranges accordingly, continuing, on a small scale, the processes of millennia past.

5

Physical Environment of the Park

Climate

Several long-standing weather stations have been maintained in Yellowstone National Park. These stations, however, are restricted to lower elevation sites and are influenced by rain shadow and cold air drainage effects. (At night, heat is radiated to space from the ground surface and the vegetation, dropping their temperature below that of the air. The air is then cooled as heat is transferred from it to the vegetation and soil. This cooler air is dense; therefore it runs down the hills and along the stream drainages, collecting in the valleys in deep pools and slow moving "rivers." This phenomenon is called cold air drainage. It is often felt as a cool evening breeze in the summer.) Only the data from these stations were available to earlier efforts to classify the climatic regimes of the Yellowstone region. On the basis of these data, the park was divided into as many as three different climatic types that grouped these stations with other low-elevation stations around the park (1).

Within the last 10 to 15 years, recording devices have been installed at higher elevations on remote snow-monitoring equipment (SNOTEL), making precipitation information available year-round from several remote stations in and around the park (2). Temperature information is also available for three to four years for some stations. These stations provide new tools for understanding the climatic regimes of the park.

Yellowstone's climate can be divided into four seasons, although some would argue that spring is just an interspersion of summer and winter days. Winter is by far the longest season. The start of winter, characterized by daily maximum temperatures frequently below freezing and the beginning of snow accumulation, comes in mid- to late October. It lasts to late March or early April. Spring, characterized by melting snow, cool to cold nights, and warm to cool days, usually begins in March or April and extends through June. Summer, characterized by warm days, frequent thunderstorms, and very infrequent freezing nighttime temperatures, lasts only through July and August. By September, freezing nighttime temperatures and warm to cool days signal the beginning of fall, which lasts through middle to late October.

In the discussions that follow, much use will be made of statistical procedures to demonstrate the relationships of factors, especially the relationship of some weather factors to elevation. A complete knowledge of statistics is not needed to understand the discussion, but a couple of definitions will prove helpful. Statisticians use an analytical method called regression to describe how two or more factors may be related. They calculate a value called r^2 to determine how close this relationship is. An r^2 value of 1.00 shows perfect correlation. If the values of two perfectly correlated factors are plotted as x- and y-coordinates all the points will fall along a straight line. This straight line is known as a regression line. Lower r^2 values indicate that the two factors are not as closely related or that they cannot be measured accurately, and the graphed points will be scattered away from the regression line. The slope of the regression line indicates how quickly one factor changes in relation to another. Both steepness and direction of the slope are important.

Precipitation

Snow is the most common form of precipitation in the park. SNOTEL data are available for two series of stations of low-intermediate and high elevations, one along the west boundary and one near the northeast corner, providing an estimate of the relationship of elevation to snowpack behavior (Table 8).

The date at which snow begins to accumulate is related to elevation. Snow begins to accumulate about October 5 at 9,000 feet. This event occurs progressively later at lower elevations, at the rate

TABLE 8
Relationship of snowcover parameters to elevation

Cover parameter	Date at 7,000 ft.	Date at 9,000 ft.	Rate of change (days/1,000 ft.)	r^2
Begin snow accumulation	Oct. 23	Oct. 5	−8.98	0.778
Maximum snow accumulation	Apr. 5	Apr. 25	9.62	0.789
End of snowpack	May 24	July 3	20.04	0.825
Duration of snowpack	213 days	271 days	29.02	0.784

of about nine days for every 1,000-foot drop in elevation. In the spring, the onset of snowmelt occurs about April 5 at 7,000 feet. This event occurs progressively later at higher altitudes, at the rate of about ten days for every 1,000-foot increase in elevation. However, the complete disappearance of snow progresses at the rate of 20 days for every 1,000-foot increase in elevation.

Mean duration of snowcover is about 213 days at 7,000 feet and increases with elevation at the rate of 29 days per 1,000 feet. If any area existed above 12,000 feet in the park, it would be continuously covered with snow. (Modern glaciers occur just south of Yellowstone in the Grand Teton Mountains, where elevations reach 13,770 feet and several peaks are above 12,000 feet.)

There is a relationship between elevation and maximum snow water content as approximated by water content of the snowpack on April 1. The scatter of the points in Figure 31 indicates that the relationship is not close on a parkwide basis, but there is a pattern: The western stations have consistently higher water content than the eastern stations. For example, Black Bear and Whiskey Creek stations on the west side have water contents similar to Fisher Creek and White Lake stations on the east side, even though the east-side stations are about 1,000 feet higher. The western stations are close to the upper regression line and the eastern stations are close to the lower regression line, indicating a closer relationship of elevation and maximum snowpack if location is considered (3).

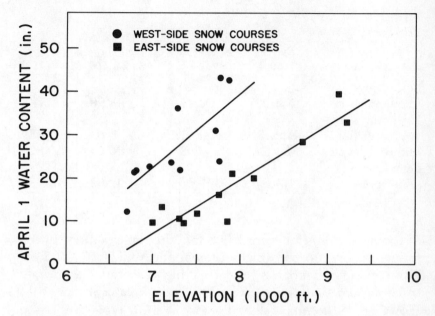

Figure 31. Relationship of snow water content on April 1 to elevation.

Eastern courses include Fisher Creek, White Mill, Northeast Entrance, Cooke Station, Canyon, Lupine Creek, Norris Basin, East Entrance, Sylvan Pass, Lake Yellowstone, Thumb Divide, and Two Ocean Plateau. Western courses include Black Bear, Whiskey Creek, Madison Plateau, West Yellowstone, Lewis Lake Divide, Grassy Lake, Snake River Station, Huckleberry Divide, Glade Creek, Coulter Creek, and Aster Creek.

Temperature

Air temperature at any particular place is a product of several physical processes. Air masses coming into an area bring with them a certain amount of energy that is expressed in the air's temperature and the heat used to evaporate moisture that the air holds. Air temperature changes as heat is conducted to or from the surface of the vegetation and ground. The ground is heated by the sun during the day and cooled by the radiation of heat to the cold reaches of outer space during the night. Air temperature also increases when energy is released by condensation of water to form precipitation. As well, air temperature is affected by changes in pressure. The rate of change in air temperature with elevation is called the lapse rate. As air moves downslope, it is compressed by the greater pressure it encounters, which causes an increase in temperature according to physical gas laws. The opposite is true of air moving upslope. This process causes a regular change in the temperature at the rate of 5.3°F per 1,000 feet, called the dry adiabatic lapse rate. If the air loses or gains moisture as a result of the temperature change, the heat of evaporation is involved and the temperature change is not as great (2.3°F per 1,000 feet). This is called the wet adiabatic lapse rate.

These relationships produce a strong correlation between temperature and elevation. The r^2 values shown in Table 9 indicate the strength of this relationship. If the slope of the regression line is considered to be the lapse rate, the spring and summer lapse rates are fairly close to the dry adiabatic lapse rate. As this slightly lower rate indicates, there are some other factors that influence the lapse rate. Cold air drainage produces temperature inversions (temperature increases with increasing elevation or decreases at a

TABLE 9

Relationship of mean monthly temperature to elevation *

Month	Lapse rate (°F/1,000 ft.)	r^2
January	−2.91	0.320
February	−3.90	0.583
March	−4.60	0.717
April	−5.31	0.902
May	−4.84	0.899
June	−4.31	0.871
July	−4.99	0.795
August	−4.60	0.726
September	−4.61	0.796
October	−4.66	0.732
November	−3.74	0.604
December	−4.07	0.539

*Stations used were Gardiner, MT; Yellowstone National Park, WY; Tower Falls, WY; Lamar Ranger Station, WY; Alta, ID; Crandall, WY; West Yellowstone, MT; South Entrance, WY; Northeast Entrance, MT; Old Faithful, WY; Cooke City, MT; and Lake Yellowstone, WY.

rate lower than the normal adiabatic lapse rate) when cold air is trapped below warmer air because of the difference in density. Valley minimum temperatures are therefore colder than they otherwise would be.

The low r^2 values for the core winter months also indicate the influence of cold air drainage and possibly the tension between the warmer western air and the cooler northern air along the Continental Divide. Here again, if the data are extrapolated to 12,000 feet the warmest month would have a mean temperature at or below freezing.

Temperature inversions are common in the larger valleys, occurring on 40 percent or more of the days during seven months of the year (4). Inversions persisting into the afternoon are most common during the winter months, occurring on 53 percent of the days in December. In nearly all valleys, local inversions resulting from cold air drainage are almost a daily occurrence, especially following calm, clear nights.

Daily variation in temperature (maximum minus minimum) ranges from 18–27 degrees Fahrenheit in winter to 33–45 degrees Fahrenheit in summer. Temperatures below freezing have been recorded every month of the year even at the lowest station (Gardiner, Montana, at 5,200 feet).

Geographic Influences

Yellowstone National Park is near the southeastern edge of a large mountainous area. It is separated from the Pacific Ocean (where air masses become charged with moisture by evaporation from the ocean surface) by 600 to 800 miles. Air masses that reach Yellowstone from the northwest must cross the Coastal Range, the Cascade Range, and the mountainous areas of northern Idaho and western Montana. Air masses that approach from the southwest must cross the Sierra Nevada Range and the basin and range country of Nevada and Utah before reaching the Yellowstone plateau. The only low-elevation approach for air masses from the west is up the Columbia River–Snake River plain (5). These air masses are stripped of much of their moisture as they rise over the Coastal and Cascade ranges. Moist air masses from the Gulf of Mexico must follow a long, circuitous route across the Great Plains to reach Yellowstone (approximately 1,500 miles). Yellowstone also straddles the Continental Divide. Deep, cold, dry continental air masses from the Arctic pushing south across the Great Plains often flow southward up the Yellowstone River Valley into the northern part of the park. Winter weather in Yellowstone typically depends on the relative strength and position of the air masses from the Pacific and the Arctic.

Figure 32 is a cross section of the Yellowstone region from Island Park, Idaho, to the divide above Cooke City, Montana. This line passes near six stations that form two elevational transects (one on the west side and one on the east side) and is in the general direction of the prevailing wind. Climatic diagrams are shown below the cross section. In each climatic diagram the horizontal axis indicates one year with a tic mark at each month, starting on the left vertical axis with January and ending on the right vertical axis with December. The vertical axes indicate mean monthly precipitation and temperature. The tics are 20 cm and 10 degrees centigrade apart, with 0 at the horizontal axis. The upper curve shows the course of mean monthly precipitation and the lower curve shows the course of mean monthly temperature. When no temperature records are available, only the precipitation curve is shown. The number below the station name is elevation in feet. This figure demonstrates the interception of precipitation on the west side, the decrease of precipitation toward the interior, and the increase again where the eastern mountains protrude above the crest of the western plateaus.

Two major climatic types are shown in Figure 33: a valley type with peak precipitation coming in the spring and a mountain type with peak precipitation in the winter. The valley climatic type is common to the large valleys and central plateaus. The mountain climatic type occurs along the Continental Divide and on its western slopes in the southern and southwestern portion of the park and in the upper portions of the mountains along the eastern and northwestern sections, where the Absaroka and Gallatin ranges protrude above the western crest lines. The mountain climate is characterized by high winter precipitation similar to the climate found along the western coastal areas (6). The colder temperatures and lower total precipitation of the park are the major difference

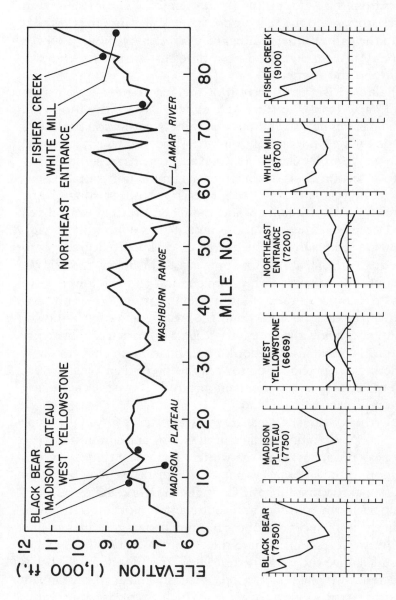

Figure 32. Topographic cross section from Island Park, Idaho, to the divide north of Cooke City, Montana, with climatic diagrams for nearby stations (see text for explanation of the graphs).

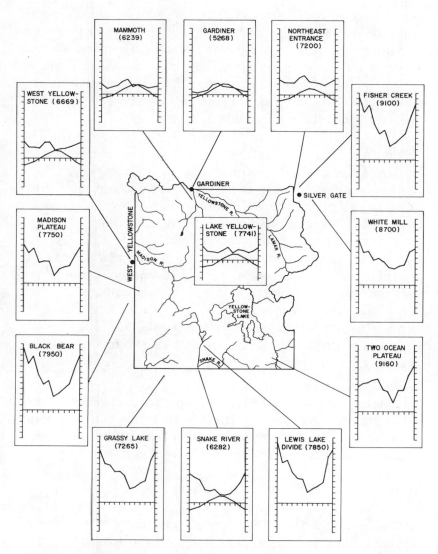

Figure 33. Climatic diagrams for selected SNOTEL and climatic stations in and near Yellowstone National Park (see text for explanation of the graphs).

between conditions of the coastal stations and Yellowstone's mountain stations. Here, 75 percent to 85 percent of the annual precipitation comes as snow or falls on snowpack. The interior stations experience a climate most similar to that of the Great Plains to the east and the intermountain region to the west, with peak precipitation in May and June. These stations receive 35 percent to 55 percent of their precipitation as rain.

These two climates leave their mark on the vegetation (7). The Yellowstone-Lamar river valleys are generally covered by dry grasslands and sagebrush steppe communities with Douglas-fir on the north-facing slopes, similar to the vegetation of comparable elevations east of the park. Like the mountains to the west, Yellowstone's mountains are generally covered by conifer forest or moist meadows, except the park has fewer conifer species. This difference may result from the park's colder temperatures and periodic extended droughts. Another exception occurs in the central part of the park, which has coarse soils derived from decomposed rhyolite. These soils generally support dry lodgepole pine communities. Even there, wherever fine soils such as those derived from lake deposits are present, sagebrush communities are also common.

Climatic Change

The climate just described is based on measurements of weather conditions averaged over the last 20 to 30 years. The measured parameters are listed as averages. It does not take much experience to know that average conditions are seldom, if ever, met; it is always warmer or colder than "normal." Departures from "normal" conditions are the rule, not the exception.

Climate is constantly changing and does so on several time scales. The geological record shows climatic changes on the scale of millions of years. Yellowstone has been under climatic conditions ranging from arctic to subtropical during its terrestrial existence (see Chapter 4).

Pollen analyses of bogs and shallow ponds in the park show climatic changes on a scale of thousands of years. Following the retreat of the glaciers (beginning about 14,000 years ago), Yellowstone's pollen sources indicate a warming trend followed by a cooling trend. Tundra conditions gave way to whitebark pine/subalpine fir forests and eventually to a strong preponderance of lodgepole pine. Timberline rose from near 4,000 to higher than 10,000 feet. Finally, about 4,000 years ago mean annual temperature began to drop and the climate cooled to its present conditions (8).

Climatic changes also occur at intervals of hundreds of years. From about 1450 to 1860, world climate was sufficiently cooler and wetter to allow new glaciers to form and existing ones to grow. Some existing glaciers in Europe advanced enough to overrun towns. Such conditions must have influenced the plant communities in Yellowstone. Most of our present forests became established during that period, and it is not safe to assume that areas disturbed today would be colonized by forests exactly like those destroyed.

Other climatic changes occur on a decade scale, such as the drought of the 1930s and the high precipitation of the 1940s. These types of trends have occurred for at least the past 230 years, as indicated by tree-ring analysis (9). The period of about 1870–1900 was considerably wetter than the present, and in the 1840s and 1850s dry conditions occurred similar to those of the 1930s but possibly more severe. Tree rings from near Mammoth Hot Springs also indicate a wet period in the mid-1830s that was preceded by about 30 years of drought.

Perhaps most noticeable to us are variations on an annual time scale. Annual precipitation for Mammoth Hot Springs is shown in Figure 34, indicating the year-to-year fluctuations that have occurred in that parameter alone.

Climate is never constant and the vegetation is always responding to the changes. In the short term, the most obvious change in vegetation is the change in plant biomass. In the longer term, there are changes in species composition of the plant communities.

Geology

The topographic setting upon which Yellowstone lies is primarily a complex of uplifted mountains of sedimentary rocks and the aftermath of two major volcanic events (10). The park straddles the point of contact of three major physiographic provinces (11). Most of the park is within the Middle Rocky Mountain Province,

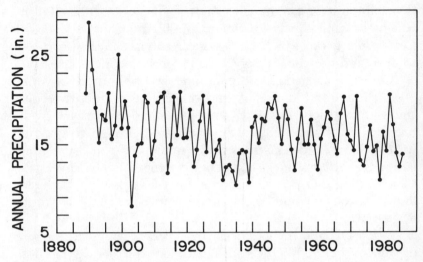

Figure 34. Annual precipitation at Mammoth Hot Springs, 1889 to 1986

characterized by mountains of uplifted blocks with large intervening basins. Sedimentary rocks are found on the flanks of the mountains, while granitic rocks are exposed near the summits. Occupying the northwest corner of the park and continuing to the north and northwest is the Northern Rocky Mountain Province, characterized by high, steep mountains and narrow basins composed primarily of sedimentary rocks. Bordering the park on the west and continuing farther to the west and southwest is the Basin and Range Province, with numerous mountain blocks and medium to large intermountain basins. Most of these mountains were formed on tension faults.

Until the late Cretaceous Era, the Yellowstone area was covered from time to time by the great continental seas of the North American Cordillera. But for the last 80 million years it has been a terrestrial environment. The Laramide orogeny uplifted three large blocks in the region: the Beartooth uplift northeast of the park, the Targhee uplift southwest of the park, and the ancestral Gallatin uplift northwest of the park. Ancestral forms of the Washakie and Teton ranges were just south of the park area.

During Eocene times, volcanic activity in two semiparallel chains produced volcanic mountains in the north and along the present east boundary of the park. This activity produced mostly andesitic rocks that weather to soils high in plant nutrients.

During Pliocene times, the Teton Range to the south arose and the Gallatin Range took on its present dimensions. A mountain range probably extended from the present Mount Sheridan in southern Yellowstone to either near or contiguous with the Gallatin Range. The Washakie Range arose to the southeast.

During Quaternary times, a large caldera exploded in the central part of the park leaving behind the lower one-third of a large volcanic mountain, the present-day Mount Washburn, and destroying most of the mountain range north of Mount Sheridan as well as the northern tip of the Washakie Range. The ashflows and later lava flows were rhyolitic in composition and are very poor in plant nutrients. The postcaldera activity has produced the high plateau nature of the southwest and central portions of the park.

Soils

Soils play an integral part in determining the types of plant communities that can grow in an area, because they are the reservoir for both plant mineral nutrients and available moisture. The amount and timing of these factors are largely responsible for determining the vegetation pattern of the park.

Soils are the product of some interesting physical and biological processes. Water leaches soluble material and clay from the upper layers and deposits them lower down. Dead leaves and roots and other biological materials are decomposed by soil microorganisms, producing organic acids and causing accumulation of organic matter in the upper layers. Organic acids dissolve the soil particles, reducing their size and releasing mineral nutrients. These processes form more or less distinctive layers called soil horizons with characteristic features that distinguish them from other horizons. The longer the processes operate, the better developed the soil becomes.

Soil particles are divided into three size classes: sand, silt, and clay. These particles are important in holding water against the forces of gravity as well as in holding ions of mineral nutrients and making them available to the roots. Water is held on the surface of the particles by intermolecular forces. The closer the water molecule is to the surface, the tighter it is held. The amount of water held in the soil is called the water-holding capacity. The chemical nature of the particle surface is important for holding dissolved nutrients and preventing them from being leached away by water. The capacity of the soil to hold these nutrients is called the cation exchange capacity.

There are two major parent materials for soil in the park: rhyolitic material and andesitic material. Both are derived from underlying bedrocks that were deposited by the two major volcanic events described in Chapter 4. Sedimentary rocks, exposed in about 6 percent of Yellowstone, are generally Paleozoic in age and are composed mostly of limestone, sandstone, and shales.

During the Ice Age, the potential existed for these various materials to be mixed; however, most of the Yellowstone area was covered by ice caps rather than overrun by glaciers. Thus the tills, the jumble of soil and rocks produced beneath moving ice deposits, were not transported very far. The soil parent material, for the most part, is derived from the underlying bedrock. There are a few exceptions. The valleys of the Lamar River and the lower Yellowstone River were filled by a large glacier, and deep layers of till were deposited. These tills are a mixture of andesite and some sedimentary rocks. Large granitic boulders, carried by the glacier, are scattered around the valley floors. Some areas to the west of the Gallatin Range also had local glaciation that deposited tills of mixed sedimentary and andesitic origin over some rhyolitic rocks.

A third factor appears to be locally significant in determining the characteristics of the soils of Yellowstone. During glacial episodes, ground-up rocks from beneath glaciers and, to some extent, from beneath ice caps were carried out by meltwater and deposited in the flood plains of the rivers. The particle size of this material was such that wind could easily pick it up and deposit it in another place. This windblown material is called loess. The distribution and duration of ice had a strong influence on the final distribution of loess across the Yellowstone landscape.

Samples of each soil horizon from 67 soil pits were gathered and analyzed during a study of Yellowstone soils (12). These pits represented the major parent materials from which the soils were derived. The results of these analyses are summarized in Table 10. Soil pits are sampled by horizon. To make meaningful comparisons of the

TABLE 10
Soil textures

Parent material	Sand (%)	Silt (%)	Clay (%)	Organic carbon (%)
Rhyolite				
High silt				
Mean	42.68	46.79	10.54	1.65
Standard error	2.39	1.75	0.86	0.22
Percent of mean	6	4	8	13
Number of pits	14	14	14	14
Low silt				
Mean	67.41	25.72	6.87	1.11
Standard error	1.76	1.70	0.47	0.23
Percent of mean	3	7	7	21
Number of pits	13	13	13	13
Andesite				
Mean	43.75	40.32	15.93	2.69
Standard error	2.67	3.16	1.27	0.36
Percent of mean	6	8	8	13
Number of pits	18	18	18	18
Mean of forested habitat types	42.05	43.04	14.91	2.36
Mean of nonforested habitat types	38.90	40.98	19.89	2.71
Glacial outwash				
Mean	53.50	34.64	11.57	1.43
Standard error	7.55	5.44	2.85	0.30
Percent of mean	14	16	25	21
Number of pits	7	7	7	7
Mixed bedrock till				
Mean	44.26	38.15	17.58	1.57
Standard error	4.23	2.44	2.97	0.11
Percent of mean	10	6	17	7
Number of pits	5	5	5	5
Miscellaneous parent material				
Thermally altered till	41.12	43.80	14.76	7.27
Andesitic thermal explosion	36.16	43.77	20.07	1.78
Lacustrine sediments	33.01	54.40	12.52	1.36
Yellowstone Lake sediments	84.96	10.64	4.40	0.59
Yellowstone Lake sediment over till	24.38	47.20	28.42	2.77
Limestone till pit #1*	33.78	46.99	19.23	3.14
Limestone till pit #2	47.47	35.48	17.05	2.50

*There were only two pits in this parent material; hence, rather than an average, the figures for both pits are given.

various soils, a weighted average was calculated for each of the soil parameters across the biologically active layer. The biologically active layer was considered to be the horizons that contained several roots. The value for each soil parameter was multiplied by the depth of the horizon and then the results were added together for each of the horizons in the active layer. This sum was then divided by the total depth of the active layer, producing the weighted average (13).

Texture

Soils derived from rhyolite contain about half as much clay as the andesitic soils. The proportion of silt is comparable in both types, but rhyolitic soils are more than half sand while andesitic soils are less than half sand (Table 10). When the percent of silt content of the 27 samples from rhyolitic soils is plotted by 5 percent size classes (Figure 35), there are two distinct peaks, one at about 40 percent and another at 20 percent. This would indicate· that either there are two types of rhyolite or something else is influencing the parent material. The mean for all rhyolitic samples is about midway between these two points, so, for analytical purposes, the rhyolitic samples were divided into two groups.

One group contained samples that fell above the average and the other those that fell below the average. The percent of clay is nearly the same in each of the types, indicating that there is probably not much difference in the type of rhyolite from which the soils were derived. Inspection of those samples in the high-silt group indicates that they are all from the unglaciated west side of the park, high elevations, or thermal areas. This would be consistent with the distribution of loess because the higher elevations and the thermal areas would be the first areas exposed in a receding ice mass. It appears that loess indeed influences some of Yellowstone's soils.

Nutrients

Andesitic rocks are richer in plant nutrients than rhyolitic rocks. For example, calcium is about ten times more abundant in andesite. It follows, then, that andesitic soils are richer in extractable macronutrients (those nutrients needed in relatively large amounts by plants) than rhyolitic soils (Table 11). Organic carbon is three times

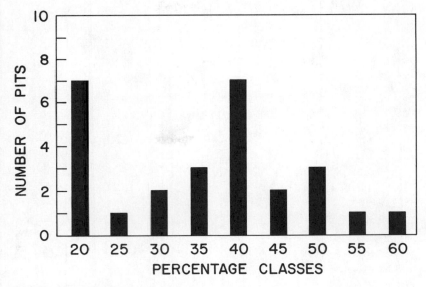

Figure 35. Silt content of rhyolitic soils

as abundant in andesitic soils. This together with the higher clay content provides for a higher cation exchange capacity. On average, the total nutrient content of andesitic soils is four times greater than that of rhyolitic soils not influenced by loess. The loess-influenced soils have half again as much mineral nutrient content as the other rhyolitic soils, but they still have much less than the andesitic soils.

Soil Moisture

Moisture enters the soil as a result of precipitation. Some water is lost from the soil by evaporation from the soil surface, but most of it is lost through absorption by the roots of plants followed by evaporation from their leaves.

In Yellowstone's climate, precipitation that starts its journey from the atmosphere to the soil in November often does not complete its trip until April or May because the entire winter's precipitation is held in the snowpack and released over a short period during spring snowmelt. Snowmelt saturates the soil, and the excess moisture either runs off in the spring freshets of the creeks and rivers

TABLE 11
Soil nutrient properties

Parent material	meq¹/100 g			
	Total Nitrogen	Ca	Sum of cations	Acidity
Rhyolite				
High silt				
Mean	0.073	2.9	15.0	10.9
Standard error	0.012	0.4	1.1	1.2
Percent of mean	16	14	7	11
Number of plots	13	14	14	14
Low silt				
Mean	0.048	2.2	9.5	6.8
Standard error	0.006	0.31	1.13	1.16
Percent of mean	12	14	12	17
Number of plots	13	13	13	12
Andesite				
Mean	0.126	18.94	38.11	15.37
Standard error	0.021	1.63	2.21	2.12
Percent of mean	17	9	6	14
Number of plots	18	18	18	15
Mean forested habitat types	0.120	15.76	33.95	14.53
Mean nonforested habitat types	0.216	21.81	35.29	10.84
Glacial outwash				
Mean	0.113	8.3	20.3	8.5
Standard error	0.024	2.0	2.6	2.1
Percent of mean	21	24	13	24
Number of plots	7	7	7	6
Mixed bedrock till				
Mean	0.090	13.3	22.9	6.9
Standard error	0.017	2.5	2.3	1.8
Percent of mean	18	19	10	26
Number of plots	5	5	5	5
Miscellaneous parent material				
Thermally altered till	0.320	9.0	18.5	5.8
Andesitic thermal explosion	0.065	5.2	16.4	9.6
Lacustrine sediments	0.056	3.6	22.0	16.7
Yellowstone Lake sediments	0.027	3.1	7.1	2.6
Yellowstone Lake sediments over till	0.174	6.3	34.4	11.9

TABLE 11
(continued)

Parent material	meq[1]/100 g			
	Total Nitrogen	Ca	Sum of cations	Acidity
Limestone till pit #1[2]	0.233	57.2	–	–
Limestone till pit #2	0.128	13.4	18.6	2.1

[1]Milliequivalents.
[2]There were only two pits in this parent material; hence, rather than an average, the figures for both pits are given.

or sinks deep into the soil to surface later in springs and seeps during the summer. Summer precipitation comes from thunderstorms. Amounts are usually small and distribution is very spotty, thus contributing little to soil moisture.

The course of mean soil moisture during the year is shown in Figure 36. The station that provided these data is in the northeast corner of the park, and the data represent ten years of information. The vertical lines represent one standard deviation around the mean water content. Although this is only one station, it at least gives an indication of conditions to be expected in most of the park.

The year-to-year variation in water content on June 1 is quite small because each year the soil profile is saturated; however, for the remaining months there is a great deal of variation due to differences in drying conditions, plant growth conditions, and input from summer showers. Soil moisture begins to climb in the spring when snowmelt starts and begins to decline as snowmelt ends. At this site snow begins to melt about April 7 and is gone by May 18. Water is drawn from the soil at the rate of about one to two inches per month, as indicated by Figure 36.

At all but the lowest elevations, temperatures suitable for plant growth occur from June through August. However, soil moisture must be available before plants can take advantage of the full growing season. The ability of the soils to store water for the growing season was assessed using the water retention difference (a measure

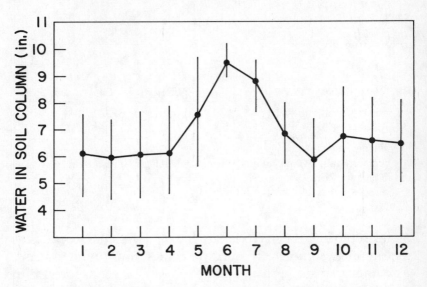

Figure 36. Ten-year average of water content of soil at Northeast Entrance at the beginning of each month, 1962–1978

Note: Vertical lines indicate standard deviation.

of the amount of water held against gravity by the soil in the field) for each soil profile. The amount of water that could be stored throughout the profile where roots were reported was also calculated. Most of the water used by the plants would come from those horizons where the roots are most common, but the deeper water can also be important to the plants. Table 12 indicates that forested andesitic soils would provide water for most if not all of the growing season, whereas the rhyolitic soils would dry out two weeks to a month before temperatures became too low for growth. The low-silt rhyolitic soils appear to have only enough surface moisture to last a month. Nonforested andesitic soils appear to be able to hold enough soil moisture to keep the vegetation green through the growing season. (This has implications for fire behavior.)

In summary, the various soil factors are strongly influenced by the bedrock from which the soils are derived, loess provides added nutrients and moisture-holding capacity to rhyolitic soils,

TABLE 12
Water-holding capacity of the soils

Parent material	Surficial[1] water retention difference (in./in.)	Surficial available water (in.)	Total available water[2] (in.)	Root depth (in.)
Rhyolite				
High silt				
Mean	0.17	4.78	9.01	31.42
Standard error	0.01	0.67	2.06	5.16
Percent of mean	10	14	23	16
Number of pits	11	11	11	12
Low silt				
Mean	0.12	3.74	8.35	32.08
Standard error	0.01	0.47	1.57	3.61
Percent of mean	10	13	19	11
Number of pits	12	13	13	13
Andesite				
Mean	0.13	6.65	9.75	47.80
Standard error	0.02	0.61	0.81	5.96
Percent of mean	12	9	8	12
Number of pits	15	14	14	14
Mean of forested habitat types	0.13	5.36	7.53	44.30
Mean of nonforested habitat types	0.15	9.99	11.52	71.25
Glacial outwash[3]				
Mean	0.14	11.58	21.75	63.33
Standard error	0.04	2.58	4.92	8.94
Percent of mean	29	22	23	14
Number of pits	6	6	6	6
Mixed bedrock till				
Mean	0.13	5.83	9.16	49.80
Standard error	0.02	0.79	1.97	8.75
Percent of mean	13	14	22	18
Number of pits	5	5	5	5
Miscellaneous parent materials				
Thermally altered till	0.33	1.66	4.36	5.00
Lacustrine sediments	0.25	6.46	23.79	26.00
Yellowstone Lake sediments	0.05	2.86	6.66	55.00

TABLE 12
(*continued*)

Parent material	Surficial[1] water retention difference (in./in.)	Surficial available water (in.)	Total available water[2] (in.)	Root depth (in.)
Yellowstone Lake sediments over till	0.23	9.52	15.04	41.00
Limestone till pit #1[4]	0.14	14.88	15.72	106.00
Limestone till pit #2	0.13	3.98	17.58	30.00

[1]Surficial horizons are those horizons with many roots. Water retention difference is a measure of the soil profile's ability to hold soil water against the force of gravity and is a function of texture, organic matter, and coarse fragments on the soil.

[2]Total available water is water held in all horizons with roots.

[3]All pits are in grassland and shrub steppe.

[4]There were only two pits in this parent material; hence, rather than an average, the figures for both pits are given.

and andesitic soils provide much better growing conditions for plants.

Correlation between Bedrock and Vegetation Types

A close look at both a vegetation map and a geology map of Yellowstone reveals that the broad vegetation pattern is related to the underlying bedrock. Certain types of vegetation are associated with andesitic mountains and others with the rhyolitic plateaus. With the advent of computers, a method of measuring this association has become available. As a part of my study, both vegetation and bedrock maps were digitized (put into a form that a computer can work with). The computer was asked to give the acreage of all possible pairs of rock type and habitat type in the park. These numbers were then used to calculate an "index of association" that relates the number of common occurrences of two things to the number of possible common occurrences (14). The index has values from +1 to −1. Zero indicates no association, the common occurrences being random events; positive values show positive association; and negative values indicate avoidance. The magnitude of the index represents the strength of the association or avoidance. The indexes for the vegetation types that cover more than 1 percent of the park are shown in Table 13.

The numbers suggest that the visual correlations on the map comparison are probably real. The drier subalpine fir and lodgepole pine types are associated with rhyolite. The strong association of the lodgepole pine/bitterbrush habitat type and Quaternary sediments results from the occurrence of the vegetation type almost exclusively on the very porous sand and gravel of a glacial outwash plain near West Yellowstone. The mesic meadows and sagebrush types are associated with the andesitic areas as are the subalpine fir/globe huckleberry habitat type and the whitebark pine phase of the subalpine fir/grouse whortleberry habitat type.

The wet vegetation types avoid both rhyolitic and andesitic bedrock types, probably because of topographic factors. They are positively associated with the Quaternary sediments. Nearly all of Yellowstone was glaciated, and so till of various depths covers the park. Areas where the till or glacial outwash is especially deep were mapped as Quaternary sediments. These sediments can be composed of either rhyolite or andesite or even a mixture of both. Glaciers leave behind a lot of potholes, which fill with water, and this probably accounts for the positive associations. The drier grass and shrubland types are also positively associated with the Quaternary sediments, but this is probably because the deeper sediments occur more commonly at the lower elevations.

The basalts and sedimentary rocks don't appear to be strongly associated with any particular vegetation types. Some of the strong negative associations probably result from the fact that basalt does not occur at high elevations, so some of the types that occur most commonly at upper elevations could not be associated with it. This elevational factor would not significantly affect the rhyolite-andesite comparison because large areas of both rock types occur at similar elevations.

TABLE 13

Cole's index of association between habitat type and bedrock type

Habitat types	Bedrock types			
	Rhyolite	Andesite	Basalt	Sedimentary rocks
Tufted hairgrass/sedges	0.346	-0.245	-0.193	-0.669
Sedge marshes	0.023	-0.700	0.254	-0.580
Idaho fescue/tufted hairgrass	0.704	-0.883		-0.123
Idaho fescue/bearded wheatgrass	-0.893	0.746	-0.620	0.006
sticky geranium phase	-0.916	0.509	-0.593	0.210
Big sagebrush/Idaho fescue	-0.735	-0.218	0.150	0.385
sticky geranium phase	-0.667	0.159	0.053	0.251
Talus and rock rubble	-0.092	0.708	-0.981	0.056
Subalpine fir/twinflower	-0.445	0.317	-0.784	0.065
Wet forest habitat types	0.274	-0.225	-0.409	-0.364

Wet forest habitat types–subalpine fir/grouse whortleberry			
grouse whortleberry phase	0.916	-0.876		-0.997
Subalpine fir/globe huckleberry	-0.388	0.176	0.008	0.107
Subalpine fir/globe huckleberry–wet forest habitat types	-0.709	0.313		0.248
Subalpine fir/western meadowrue	-0.720	0.183	-0.879	0.355
Subalpine fir/pinegrass	0.261	-0.822	0.231	-0.703
Subalpine fir/Geyer's sedge	0.995	-0.995	-0.982	
Subalpine fir/grouse whortleberry				
whitebark pine phase	-0.550	0.474	-1.000	-0.017
pinegrass phase	0.685	-0.911		0.004
grouse whortleberry phase	0.775	-0.795	-0.031	-0.956
Subalpine fir/Ross's sedge	0.995		-0.939	
Whitebark pine/grouse whortleberry	-0.431	0.519	-0.580	
Lodgepole pine/bitterbrush	-0.211		0.523	
Douglas-fir/pinegrass	0.056	-0.440	0.111	-0.080
Douglas-fir/snowberry	-0.070	-0.031	0.056	0.476

Generally speaking, the types that are strongly associated with rhyolite either avoid or are not as strongly associated with andesite. The bases for these relationships are undoubtedly rooted in the soil. The previous section documents the differences in the soils derived from these two parent materials.

Relationships between bedrock and vegetation produce some interesting contrasts. Plant communities can be quite different at equivalent elevations depending on whether they are on rhyolitic or andesitic soil. In Yellowstone, andesitic substrates have a much higher incidence of meadows; rhyolitic substrates are covered with a nearly continuous forest.

The higher mineral nutrition available from andesitic rocks permits higher plant production, which in turn provides more available food for animal populations. It is no coincidence that the summer ranges used most heavily by the ungulates of the park are on the andesitic mountains or that grizzly bears spend most of their foraging time in vegetation associated with andesitic substrates. Hayden and Pelican valleys, in the middle of the rhyolite plateaus, might at first appear to be exceptions to this generality, but these valleys are on glacial lake sediments derived largely from andesitic rocks.

The interrelationship of geology and plant cover makes possible the division of the park into different units of landscape with common topographic and vegetational characteristics. These units are here called geovegetation provinces, in recognition of the basis of the division. These provinces are the subject of the next chapter.

6

Descriptions of the Geovegetation Provinces

Yellowstone can be divided into five geologic-climatic provinces: Gallatin Range, Absaroka Range, Central Plateaus, Southwest Plateaus, and Yellowstone-Lamar Valleys (Fig. 37). These provinces each have a characteristic bedrock type that has produced a particular group of soils. The bedrock types also produce topography that in turn produces characteristic microclimates. This results in distinctive combinations of habitat types.

Gallatin Range

The Gallatin Range Province is located in the northwest quadrant and occupies 7 percent of the park. It is underlain by a combination of andesitic Absaroka volcanics and sedimentary rocks. Peaks rise above timberline (which is near 9,400 feet) to 11,000 feet. The bases of the mountains are about 7,200 feet. Annual precipitation averages between 50 and 60 inches along the crests to 40 inches at the base. Topography is well dissected with deep, steep-sided valleys and some rounded ridgetops.

The rocks weather to soils with a high clay content and good water-holding capacity. Mineral nutrient levels are relatively high, providing good plant growth. Too few soil pits were sampled in this province to adequately document the soils' characteristics, but it can be inferred from the pits dug and the rock types of the province that the soils would be similar to those of the Absaroka Range Province.

This province is 75 percent forested (Table 14). Habitat types most commonly encountered are subalpine fir/western meadow-

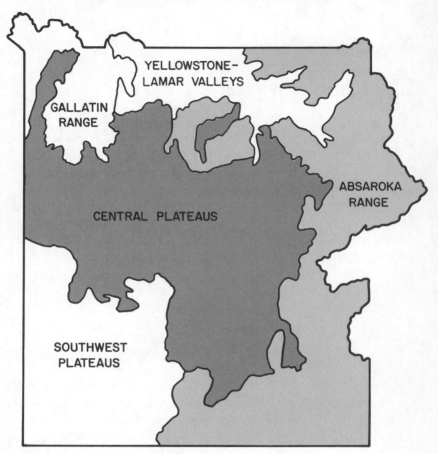

Figure 37. Geovegetation provinces

rue, the whitebark pine phase of the subalpine fir/grouse whortleberry habitat type, and the sticky geranium phase of the Idaho
fescue/bearded wheatgrass habitat type. Spruce-fir and whitebark
pine forests are common in the higher elevations. Douglas-fir is
common at lower elevations, where it occurs most frequently in
the Douglas-fir/pinegrass habitat type.

Absaroka Range

The Absaroka Range Province occupies the park's eastern edge
and southeastern quarter and comprises 32 percent of the park's

TABLE 14

Habitat types covering more than 1 percent of the Gallatin Range Province

Habitat type	Percentage of province	Percentage of habitat type
Subalpine fir/twinflower	5.7	21.5
Wet forest types	3.4	3.0
Subalpine fir/globe huckleberry	1.1	1.3
Subalpine fir/western meadowrue	29.0	39.9
Subalpine fir/grouse whortleberry		
whitebark pine phase	22.3	14.7
pinegrass phase	1.4	6.4
grouse whortleberry phase	8.1	2.0
Whitebark pine/grouse whortleberry	1.2	6.1
Douglas-fir/pinegrass	1.7	7.9
Douglas-fir/snowberry	1.3	3.5
Tufted hairgrass/sedge	1.6	5.3
Idaho fescue/bearded wheatgrass	1.3	29.1
sticky geranium phase	9.4	16.8
Big sagebrush/Idaho fescue		
sticky geranium phase	4.1	7.9
Talus and rock rubble	5.4	22.3
Total forested habitat types	75.3	
Total nonforested habitat types	24.7	

area. Absaroka volcanics predominate, but there are islands of rhyolite scattered throughout and an occasional outcrop of sedimentary rock along the southern boundary. Elevations range from 6,600 to 7,700 feet at the western bases to 11,000 feet along its divide. This divide forms most of the park's eastern boundary. Precipitation in these mountains is similar to that of the Madison Range, averaging between 50 and 60 inches along the crests and 30 inches near the base. Precipitation is lower here than at equivalent elevations in the Madison Range or Southwest Plateaus. Topography is dominated by deep, steep-sided valleys with highly erodible slopes.

Soils average 14 percent clay and 41 percent silt. This provides good water-holding capacity and mineral nutrient content, nearly three times that of soils on the rhyolitic plateaus.

The province is 77 percent forested (Table 15). The most com-

TABLE 15

Habitat types covering more than 1 percent of the Absaroka Range Province

Habitat type	Percentage of province	Percentage of habitat type
Subalpine fir/twinflower	3.6	58.2
Wet forest types	9.6	37.3
Subalpine fir/globe huckleberry	15.2	74.3
Subalpine fir/western meadowrue	7.4	43.7
Subalpine fir/pinegrass	1.9	13.7
Subalpine fir/grouse whortleberry	1.9	13.7
whitebark pine phase	24.6	70.1
grouse whortleberry phase	8.8	9.7
Whitebark pine/grouse whortleberry	3.7	83.6
Douglas-fir/snowberry	1.4	17.1
Alpine tundra	1.9	90.3
Tufted hairgrass/sedge meadow	3.0	42.0
Idaho fescue/bearded wheatgrass	0.5	44.4
sticky geranium phase	8.4	64.2
Willow bottoms	1.1	65.9
Big sagebrush/Idaho fescue		
sticky geranium phase	2.4	19.8
Talus and rock rubble	4.0	71.8
Total forested habitat types	77.4	
Total nonforested habitat types	22.6	

mon forested habitat types are the whitebark pine phase of the subalpine fir/grouse whortleberry and subalpine fir/globe huckleberry habitat types. Spruce-fir forests are a common cover type; however, lodgepole pine forests are most common. Whitebark pine is a common cover type above 8,600 feet. Nonforest habitat types are largely Idaho fescue/bearded wheatgrass habitat type in the sticky geranium phase. Large areas of cliff and talus occur in this province.

Central Plateaus

The Central Plateaus Province comprises 34 percent of the park's area and is underlain by Quaternary rhyolite. Elevations are generally about 8,200 feet. Precipitation ranges between 20 and

40 inches over a large portion of the province. Topography, for the most part, consists of nearly flat, undulating plateaus occasionally cut by canyons.

The rocks weather to a coarse, sandy soil (60 percent sand, 9 percent clay) with poor water-holding capacity and low plant nutrient levels (only a third of that of soils from the andesitic mountains).

Forested habitat types cover 90 percent of the province (Table 16) and are mostly subalpine fir/grouse whortleberry habitat type in the grouse whortleberry phase, with a good representation of drier subalpine fir types. Lodgepole pine covers most of the area, but some spruce-fir stands can be found, mostly where wet forests occupy the province. Nonforested types cover little area (10 percent) and are mostly wet grassland and shrubland types in areas where fine-grained alluvium occurs. Soils of the nonforested types are considerably higher in silt plus clay (44 percent) than those of the forested types (16 percent).

TABLE 16

Habitat types covering more than 1 percent of the Central Plateaus Province

Habitat type	Percentage of province	Percentage of habitat type
Wet forest types	10.0	42.2
Subalpine fir/western meadowrue	1.8	11.5
Subalpine fir/pinegrass	6.4	49.0
Subalpine fir/elk sedge	6.8	89.5
Subalpine fir/grouse whortleberry		
pinegrass phase	4.1	85.2
grouse whortleberry phase	51.3	61.0
Lodgepole pine/bitterbrush	3.8	100.0
Douglas-fir/pinegrass	2.3	49.4
Tufted hairgrass/sedge	2.3	35.0
Hot ground types	1.1	94.1
Silver sage/Idaho fescue	2.1	98.2
Big sagebrush/Idaho fescue		
sticky geranium phase	2.4	21.2
Sedge marshes	1.4	42.6
Total forested habitat types	89.5	
Total nonforested habitat types	10.5	

Southwest Plateaus

The Southwest Plateaus Province occupies 18 percent of the park. Most of the park's southwestern quarter is underlain by some of the most recent rhyolitic flows in the park. Elevations are near 8,800 feet at the crests and range between 6,500 and 7,200 feet at the bases. Basalt flows also cover a significant portion. Precipitation is highest in this region, estimated to be from 40 inches at the bases to 70 inches at the crests. Topography consists of nearly flat, undulating plateaus cut by occasional canyons.

The rocks weather to a coarse, sandy soil with poor water-holding capacity and low mineral nutrient levels. The soils on the western portion of the province are influenced by windblown material, with 50 percent of the soil consisting of silt. This characteristic gives the soil higher nutrient content than soils on other areas underlain by rhyolite.

The most common forested types are subalpine fir/grouse whortleberry habitat type in the grouse whortleberry phase with a good representation of the whitebark pine phase, subalpine fir/Ross's sedge habitat type, and subalpine fir/pinegrass habitat type (Table 17). Most cover types are dominated by lodgepole pine.

TABLE 17
Habitat types covering more than 1 percent of the Southwest Plateaus Province

Habitat type	Percentage of province	Percentage of habitat type
Wet forest types	7.4	16.4
Subalpine fir/globe huckleberry	7.5	20.9
Subalpine fir/pinegrass	8.6	34.5
Subalpine fir/elk sedge	1.1	7.9
Subalpine fir/grouse whortleberry		
whitebark pine phase	7.3	11.9
grouse whortleberry phase	43.4	27.1
Subalpine fir/Ross's sedge	9.2	96.7
Whitebark pine/elk sedge	3.4	80.3
Tufted hairgrass/sedge	1.1	72.5
Pitchstone Plateau complex	5.3	100.0
Sedge marshes	1.7	27.7
Total forested habitat types	88.9	
Total nonforested habitat types	11.1	

Nonforested types are largely Idaho fescue/tufted hairgrass with some tufted hairgrass/sedge types. An unusual vegetation pattern called the Pitchstone Plateau complex covers the higher elevations of this area. Whitebark pine, Engelmann spruce, and subalpine fir occupy the ridges that were produced by flowing lava while Idaho fescue and tufted hairgrass occupy the intervening depressions.

Yellowstone-Lamar River Valleys

In the north-central part of the park lie the large valleys of the Yellowstone and Lamar rivers, occupying 9 percent of the park. These valleys are largely filled with glacial debris of andesitic volcanic and sedimentary composition. Elevations here are the lowest in the park, ranging from 5,200 feet (at North Entrance) to about

TABLE 18

Habitat types covering more than 1 percent of the Yellowstone-Lamar River Valleys Province

Habitat type	Percentage of province	Percentage of habitat type
Subalpine fir/twinflower	2.4	10.5
Wet forest types	1.0	1.0
Subalpine fir/western meadowrue	3.0	4.8
Subalpine fir/pinegrass	1.4	2.6
Subalpine fir/grouse whortleberry		
whitebark pine phase	1.4	7.4
Douglas-fir/pinegrass	6.6	34.9
Douglas-fir/shiny-leaf spirea	1.1	97.6
Douglas-fir/mallow ninebark	1.0	94.6
Douglas-fir/snowberry	23.7	76.4
Tufted hairgrass/sedge	2.3	8.8
Idaho fescue/bearded wheatgrass	1.7	67.6
sticky geranium phase	8.6	17.6
Big sagebrush/Idaho fescue	14.4	82.8
sticky geranium phase	22.9	51.1
Sedge marshes	1.0	7.4
Total forested habitat types	44.0	
Total nonforested habitat types	56.0	

6,500 feet. Precipitation is also lowest, ranging from 11 to 20 inches. Topography of the valley bottoms is undulating, often with contorted drainage resulting from glacial depositions. Rocks weather to soils with high water-holding capacity and high levels of plant mineral nutrients.

Most of this zone is covered by nonforested types (Table 18). The big sagebrush series covers 37 percent of the area. Big sagebrush/Idaho fescue habitat type in the sticky geranium phase predominates. However, grasslands of both phases of the Idaho fescue/bearded wheatgrass habitat type cover 10 percent of the province. Forested types are dominated by Douglas-fir and are mostly of the Douglas-fir/snowberry or Douglas-fir/pinegrass types.

Disturbance and Succession

Disturbance is ubiquitous in vegetation and is a natural process in all ecosystems. The Yellowstone vegetation is subjected to many natural disturbances. Fire is the most obvious type of disturbance, but forests and other vegetation are also subject to periodic outbreaks of insects and diseases as well as infrequent extreme winds, avalanches, water table changes, climatic changes, and changes in geothermal outputs.

Disturbances differ greatly in frequency, extent of occurrence, and severity of impact. But vegetation is very resilient. Immediately following a disturbance, a plant community develops from the plants that survived. Plants can survive as unaffected individuals, seed, or belowground parts capable of regenerating. A few new species invade to occupy some of the sites left vacant by the killed plants and the long, often slow process of reinvasion by species that were eliminated by the disturbance begins.

The environment at the soil's surface is not the same as it was before the disturbance. Much more light reaches the soil surface, resulting in higher soil-surface temperatures during the day. Lower temperatures occur at night as energy radiates into outer space directly from the soil surface rather than from the tree tops. Thus, temperature range increases. A forest canopy intercepts a significant portion of the precipitation that falls and allows it to evaporate before reaching the ground; snowmelt dates are altered by canopy shade. Thus, the soil water regime of a stand is significantly altered by disturbance.

Even soil nutrient levels are affected. Nutrients that would have been absorbed had the plants not been killed are made available for the plants that either survived or establish early on the site.

Fire reduces a lot of plant material to ashes. These ashes are composed mostly of inorganic compounds that are needed by the plants. During snowmelt and summer rain showers, these nutrients are leached back into the soil. In undisturbed forests, mineral nutrients from the leaves and bark of trees are dissolved in the precipitation that falls through the tree crowns and runs down the tree trunks. These nutrients, then, are deposited in the soil. This part of the nutrient balance is altered by disturbance.

In short, the site's position in multidimensional environmental space is altered, with the result that the plant community occupying the site immediately after a disturbance is different from the one that occupied the site previously. The community can change in two ways: Plant species may be different and the biomass relationships of the plant species may change.

Different species have adopted different strategies for coping with disturbance. Some specialize in survival while others specialize in rapid reoccupation. As reestablished plants grow, the site characteristics change and the plant community changes accordingly.

Perhaps the best and most widespread example in Yellowstone is the relationship of lodgepole pine, Engelmann spruce, and subalpine fir. Lodgepole pine does well in an unshaded site. It is not damaged by the higher temperatures at the soil surface and can make good use of higher light levels for photosynthesis. It does not do well at lower light levels common to the forest floor under a closed canopy because photosynthesis is relatively low. Engelmann spruce and subalpine fir, on the other hand, require cooler temperatures but can photosynthesize adequately in the shade of the overstory. Lodgepole pinecones often remain closed at maturity, a condition known as serotiny, where the cone scales are glued shut by a resin that only melts at temperatures higher than that normally reached by the air. The seeds can remain alive in the cone for years. In contrast, the seeds of both Engelmann spruce and subalpine fir are shed from the cone every year.

These differences in physiology and growth habit produce different results following a disturbance. The heat of a fire or the sunny soil surface is sufficient to melt the resin of lodgepole pinecones and release the seeds that have been stored. Lodgepole pine seedlings begin to grow immediately. With the passage of time, the lodgepole pine canopy closes in and the ground becomes completely shaded. In the meantime, Engelmann spruce and subalpine fir seedlings, which have germinated from seed blown into the opening from surrounding forests or from pockets of trees missed by the disturbance, begin to establish and form an understory. Lodgepole pine seedlings begin to be shaded out. Eventually, the number of lodgepole pine seedlings decreases while the other two species become more numerous. As the seedlings grow into the overstory, the forest changes from lodgepole pine to Engelmann spruce–subalpine fir. If another disturbance does not eliminate the spruce-fir overstory, only spruce and fir seedlings will be able to establish in the forest. In this way, the spruce and fir forest can perpetuate itself indefinitely. This Engelmann spruce–subalpine fir forest is the climax forest. This is the most common plant succession scenario in Yellowstone where soil nutrients are relatively high, soil moisture is sufficient, and temperatures are moderate.

But there are exceptions. Some sites are too dry and too low in mineral nutrients to support Engelmann spruce or subalpine fir, but they can support lodgepole pine. In these areas, lodgepole pine trees bear a large proportion of nonserotinous cones, and the crowns are usually sparse enough to allow the lodgepole pine seedlings to receive enough light to enable them to grow into the overstory. Here lodgepole pine is the climax species (1).

On warmer sites, Douglas-fir has the advantage. In areas where mineral nutrients are high, Douglas-fir forms the first postdisturbance forest as well as the climax forest. In other areas, lodgepole pine will form the first postdisturbance forest to be succeeded by Douglas-fir, but such sites are not common in Yellowstone. The largest area of this latter type is found on the rhyolite flows east of West Yellowstone, which were not covered by ice during the last glaciation. This area received a covering of windblown soil material that added nutrients to the rhyolite-derived soils, making it possible for Douglas-fir to occupy the site.

Very cold sites (such as those at higher elevations, on steep north-facing slopes, and on stream bottoms with common cold air drainage) start with climax species. Engelmann spruce and subalpine fir are able to establish on unshaded sites. Here, the successional forests are dominated by a combination of Engelmann spruce, subalpine fir, and lodgepole or whitebark pine. Whitebark pine may also form the first postdisturbance community in areas above 8,600 feet.

The time it takes for these changes to occur varies during the course of the process. Immediately after the disturbance, adjustments in the composition and condition of the vegetation begin. For instance, plants whose tops burned in a forest fire begin to resprout and grow new tops. This is especially common in grasses and forbs with deep underground rhizomes. If the fire occurs early in the summer, some plants can regrow a top, flower, and set seed before the growing season is over. In the first few years ground cover is reestablished, and the tree species begin the long process of establishment on the site. In Yellowstone, this process is more a matter of changes in biomass than of species. A spruce-fir forest may become a lodgepole pine forest, but there were a few lodgepole in the original forest and both spruce and fir seedlings establish with the lodgepole pine, albeit in very low numbers.

After the first flush of activity to reoccupy the newly available environment, the processes slow down and the number of adjustments decreases. The next major change takes place approximately 30 to 40 years later, when the tree crowns begin to shade the ground. Some of the species on the forest floor are shaded out, and the trees begin to compete with each other for the available site amenities, such as light and moisture. A period of adjustment follows wherein tree numbers change. The dense lodgepole pine stands are thinned as the most vigorous individuals outlast the less suited ones. This process may take as long as 250 years. As the lodgepole pine reach maturity and climax species begin to establish more abundantly and grow in the understory, the process slows again.

A Case Study in Tree Succession

In 1935, some forward-looking biologists established four plots in Yellowstone to study the process of succession over a long time period. One, located in an aspen stand, was destroyed by construction; another, in a wet spruce-fir forest, has not been remeasured; but the other two were remeasured in 1957, 1976, and 1985.

The two plots were in entirely different vegetation types. One was in a 190-year-old lodgepole pine stand at an elevation of 8,450 feet. The other was in a 250-year-old Douglas-fir stand at 6,400 feet. In each stand, a 1/10-acre square plot was permanently marked. Each tree was given a number, tagged, and measured and its location was recorded on a map. Trees more than one inch dbh (diameter at breast height) were cored; their age was determined and growth over the first ten and last ten years of life was measured. The height of all the smaller trees was also recorded.

The Douglas-fir stand had only seven young trees smaller than one inch dbh in 1935 and none have established in the last 50 years. More than half of the trees have died, all but one of them in the smaller size classes. Eleven of the eighteen trees that died did so during an outbreak of spruce budworm between 1976 and 1985. There was a similar outbreak in the 1950s, and the others may have died at that time. Despite the loss of so many trees, the total basal area of the stand increased by one square foot during the 50 years. (Basal area is the area of the tree trunk and is usually calculated from dbh. This value is related to the size of the crown and other ecologically important parameters.) Total basal area increased 25 percent by 1976, then dropped back to just 6 percent increase over the original value. Only one of the trees that was dead in 1957 had fallen over by 1976.

Dynamics of the 190-year-old lodgepole pine stand are much more complicated, due in part to the greater number of species involved. The stand has gained 95 new individuals in the intervening 50 years: 75 subalpine fir, 18 Engelmann spruce, and 2 whitebark pine. No lodgepole pine seedlings became established. Meanwhile, three of the small subalpine fir and two small Engelmann spruce died.

In the overstory, no subalpine fir or Engelmann spruce died, but ten lodgepole pine died. Total stand basal area increased through 1976 and then declined, just as it did in the lower elevation stand, though not by as much.

Basal area of both Engelmann spruce and subalpine fir increased throughout the 50-year period, while that of lodgepole pine decreased. One small Engelmann spruce and six small subalpine fir advanced to the greater-than-one-inch dbh size class. If this rate of change from lodgepole pine to Engelmann spruce and subalpine fir continues, it will take at least another 200 years before most of the lodgepole pine are gone.

The four plot measurements provided data for three intervals: 1935 to 1957, 1958 to 1976, and 1977 to 1985. Mean annual change in basal area of the stand appears to be related to mean annual precipitation during each interval. The plots were established in the middle of the drought of the 1930s, but the following years were wet enough that average annual precipitation during the first interval was near normal. There was little change in stand basal area. Growth of individual trees was minimal. The average annual precipitation during the second interval was nearly an inch above normal and stand basal area increased, while that during the last interval was an inch below normal and stand basal area declined. The decline in basal area was accomplished by the death of several of the smaller trees in the Douglas-fir stand. In the lodgepole stand, the adjustment was made by death of the pioneer lodgepole pine. Precipitation was recorded at Tower Junction, which is about one mile east of the lower site and five and a half miles north of the higher site. Regression analysis of these data (Fig. 38) indicates that the basal area of the stand is closely related to the mean annual precipitation during the interval.

It appears that the tree material produced during the two wetter intervals was in excess of what the soil moisture could support during the drier third interval. It is entirely possible that the insects in the Douglas-fir stand merely performed a regulating function on the Douglas-fir forests by eliminating the excess basal area during times of less favorable climatic conditions.

The lodgepole pine in the upper stand did not die from bark beetles. The cause of death was not apparent in the dead trees. Still, the basal area was adjusted in the lodgepole pine stand to accommodate the lesser precipitation. All the losses were sustained by the successional lodgepole pine rather than by the climax species.

These data demonstrate the slow pace of the successional process in Yellowstone's subalpine forests during their final stage of transforming from a lodgepole pine forest to a spruce-fir forest. This last stage is highly susceptible to all the disturbance factors

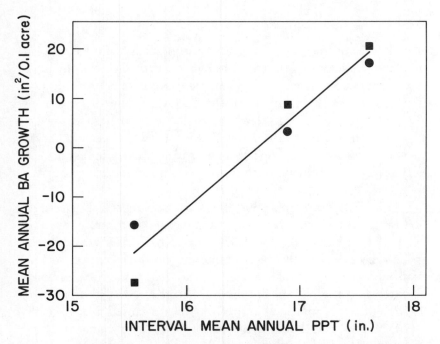

Figure 38. Relationship of mean annual precipitation (PPT) and basal area (BA) change for three intervals: 1935–1957, 1958–1976, and 1977–1985

Note: Squares designate the subalpine stand of old lodgepole pine; circles designate the montane stand of Douglas-fir.

and, for this reason, forests dominated by Engelmann spruce and subalpine fir are quite rare in the park. The data also show that tree succession in most Douglas-fir stands is from small Douglas-fir, postdisturbance, to large Douglas-fir that maintain themselves for hundreds of years.

Both these plots were burned during the fires of 1988. It is unfortunate that the same trees cannot be measured again in ten years but it will be interesting to follow the process of succession on plots where the history of the past 50 years is known.

Fire

Fire has been a part of the Yellowstone ecosystem for as long as there has been vegetation suitable to burn. Cores from bogs have produced charred needles that are thousands of years old (2). The climate has been dry since the Cascade Range arose during the Pliocene Era. An age-class map of the park forests (see cover-type map, inside back cover) reveals a fire-created mosaic that was present long before European man arrived. Fire suppression is a very recent event in the ecosystem and is generally inappropriate in a park managed as a natural area.

In 1972, nearly 300,000 acres in the central portion of Yellowstone National Park were designated, on a trial basis, as a Natural Fire Zone (3). Here lightning-caused fires were closely monitored but were allowed to burn without intervention. Information gained in these areas was used to determine the feasibility of extending the natural fire program to the rest of the park. In 1976, a plan was approved whereby lightning-caused fires in nearly all of the park could be considered for designation as natural fires and allowed to follow their normal course. Until that time, fires were suppressed for two main reasons: 1) Public-use facilities were threatened or 2) the fire had the potential to spread onto neighboring lands where total suppression was the policy (4). By 1982, the surrounding national forests had approved fire management plans in portions of their units adjacent to the park, allowing lightning-caused fires to burn under certain conditions. A memorandum of understanding between the agencies provided for discussion on allowing a given fire to burn across shared boundaries.

The fire season in Yellowstone normally lasts from early July to mid-October; it is brought to an end by a series of two- to three-day rain or snowstorms followed by cool temperatures and the eventual onset of winter conditions. Precipitation during the fire season is about 1.4 inches per month throughout the park. Rainless periods lasting 15 days or more average only one per season, with a maximum of four recorded (5). Very dry years occur occasionally. During such years, precipitation may be less than 0.6 inches for the entire fire season.

Mean maximum air temperature in the central portion of the park during the most active part of the fire season is near 72°F in July and 61°F in June and August. The highest temperature recorded since 1948 is 89°F. The prevailing wind direction is from the southwest. Wind speed at 20 feet above the ground averages 6 miles/hour or more only 7 percent of the time (6).

Records kept in the park since 1930 show that an average of 17 fires are started by lightning each year, though this number varied between 2 and 58. Early *Superintendent's Reports* mention fires that burned from midsummer until late October (7).

Suppression efforts were attempted as early as 1877 by the meager work force attempting to protect the park in the early days (8). In 1886 the U.S. Army, which was given responsibility for protection of the park at that time, became the first governmental agency to declare war on wildland fire (9). These early efforts were quite effective in the sagebrush steppe and grassland areas of the park, but detection and logistical problems limited their effectiveness in the forested areas. By the time a fire was large enough to be seen, it was well established; by the time men and equipment could be moved to the fire, it had covered many acres. In some cases suppression efforts may have kept a fire from going through a second or third active period, but most often the fire was stopped by a natural barrier or change in weather.

Increased use of aircraft and smokejumpers in the early 1950s brought much more effective detection and the ability to get men to a fire while it was small. Today, through the use of helicopters and slurry bombers, fires in the park can usually be kept relatively small if suppression is deemed appropriate.

The time between successive fires on a specific area (the return interval) in most of Yellowstone's forests is between 200 and 400 years (10). Therefore, fire suppression efforts have not yet caused a significant departure from natural conditions in the forests. Fuels have not built up to an unnatural level, and plant succession has not been allowed to proceed beyond what it would in a natural fire regime. Some areas that would have burned in the past 20 to 30 years are still in their unburned state, but these areas are relatively small and should not alter the fire regime significantly.

From 1972 to the end of the 1987 fire season, 235 fires were allowed to burn without interference. Two hundred and eight remained less than 1 acre in size; 16 burned more than 100 acres each. All but 1 of the 27 fires larger than 1 acre burned as crown fires. Since expansion of the natural fire plan to include most of the park, 134 lightning-caused fires have been suppressed for various reasons. Some of those had shown high potential for becoming large fires. Less than 40,000 acres burned in the first 15 years of this management practice. This amounts to less than 0.15 percent of the park per year. At this rate it would take about 675 years to burn all the park forests. However, the 1988 fire season showed us that natural processes do not always follow such predictable paths.

The 1979 fire season was relatively severe. Twenty-nine fires were started by lightning; 11 of these were suppressed because they had the possibility of becoming a threat to public facilities. Of the remaining 18 fires, 13 burned less than 1 acre. One lasted six weeks but burned only 20 acres. Four became large, burning a total of 10,520 acres.

The 1981 fire season was more severe. Fifty-seven fires were caused by lightning (only 1 fire short of the highest number of fires recorded in 50 years). Of those 57, 28 were allowed to burn. Fifteen remained less than 1 acre in size. A total of 20,240 acres were burned. Four fires burned more than 2,000 acres each. The Forest Lake fire near the South Entrance covered 7,396 acres.

The 1988 fire season will become legendary in Yellowstone folklore. Approximately 794,000 acres burned within the park. The nation's best efforts were insufficient to keep all the fires that started within the park inside the park boundaries. They were also inadequate to keep some human-caused fires started near the park's boundary from entering the park and burning considerable area. Eleven of the park's 15 developed areas and all three neighboring communities were threatened by fires. Six hundred miles of manually built fireline and 32 miles of bulldozed fireline needed to be restored to natural conditions when it was all over.

Within Yellowstone 10 lightning-caused fires were immediately suppressed; 27 were allowed to burn (11 of these went out on their own). Natural fires burned a total of 350,000 acres within the park; suppression action was eventually taken on those that did not go out. One of these fires threatened Grant Village and another went across the park boundary and burned 80,000 acres in the Shoshone National Forest. Suppression efforts were successful in keeping two others within the park. Two fires that were at first allowed to burn on Forest Service land eventually burned into the park, consuming 48,000 acres. Three human-caused fires also burned into the park, consuming 445,000 acres. One of these fires accounted for 406,000 acres and threatened six developments and two gateway communities. All available and appropriate suppression strategies were employed in an attempt to suppress this fire, but they proved to be inadequate.

The causes of the 1988 fire season will be researched and debated for a long time. At this point it appears that the larger number of rainless days and the number of days of high wind are the main differences between 1988 and previous extreme fire years. The fires were able to creep across areas that had burned during the past few decades. In previous years they were unable to do so. As well, fires burned under many acres of young and middle-aged lodgepole pine forests, leaving the tree crowns unburned. In previous years these stands had acted as natural fire breaks.

Table 19 lists the fires that have occurred within the original Natural Fire Zones, where all fires of the past 15 years have been allowed to burn unrestricted. These data reflect a nearly natural fire regime. More than 84 percent of the fires remained less than 5 acres in size. It is apparent that most lightning-caused fires remain very small. The conditions necessary for large crown fires, once ignition has occurred, apparently are not often met. During a normal fire year, very little area is burned by ground or surface fire in Yellowstone. The proper fuel amounts and arrangement just do not occur frequently. Fires either burn large areas as crown fires or smolder in the duff.

Once a fire reaches several acres, conditions occur that may allow it to persist through cold and wet conditions. Fires smolder in the accumulated cone scales of squirrel middens, in deep accumulations of duff and forest litter, in rotten logs, and in standing trees and snags that have dry rot.

Snowmelt each spring usually saturates these fuels. During the

TABLE 19

Number of fires that burned unrestricted within the Two Ocean and Mirror Plateau areas, 1972–1988

Year	Size class				Total fires	Total acres
	< 2.5a	2.5–12a	12–123a	>123a		
1972	2	0	0	0	2	<1
1973	2	0	0	0	2	<1
1974	2	0	2	2	6	824
1975	6	0	0	0	6	<1
1976	9	0	1	1	11	1,550
1977	1	1	0	0	2	10
1978	1	0	0	0	1	<1
1979	6	0	0	2	8	4,942
1980	1	0	0	0	1	<1
1981	6	0	2	5	13	2,095
1982	2	0	0	0	2	<1
1983	1	0	0	0	1	<1
1984	7	0	0	0	7	<1
1985	26	0	0	0	26	<1
1986	14	0	0	0	14	<1
1987	8	0	0	0	8	<1
1988	8	0	1	6	15	127,213
Total	101	1	5	10	116	136,634

dry summers, however, the fuels dry to considerable depths and are usually kept dry because the tree crowns directly above them intercept much of the light summer showers. Once ignited, these fuels smolder until they are consumed or wet fuels are encountered. If the surface fuels dry out again, the smoldering fire may ignite them and flaming fronts recur. One large fire started on July 23 and persisted until October 10, when a fall storm of snow and rain finally extinguished it. It made major runs (increased significantly in size) on July 26 and 27, which accounted for nearly three-fourths of its final size. During August, it survived some days of below normal temperature and several rain showers, even a snow shower. Most other large fires have persisted into the fall wet period.

We have learned a lot about the role of fire in Yellowstone's ecosystem and about some of the interactions between fire and the vegetation. Fires are not random events but are dependent on a special set of circumstances. The weather must be just right and the vegetation must have provided a proper amount and distribution of fuel. Most fires start when lightning strikes a large, old spruce or fir tree laden with lichens, causing the top of the tree to burn. Firebrands rain on the forest floor and those that fall into beds of dry fuel extend the fire. If there are no fuels present or the fuels are wet, the fire dies. Fire spread is also dependent on the availability and condition of fuels as well as on the weather. These concepts are illustrated in the flow diagram in Figure 39.

The physical environment of Yellowstone's forests is not conducive to the growth of tall, shrubby species, so the most common fuels on the forest floor are young trees and trees that have died and fallen. The three most common tree species in the forests are lodgepole pine, Engelmann spruce, and subalpine fir. Differences in their physiology are reflected in differences in their growth forms, and this in turn influences the fuels they produce. Lodgepole pine needles cannot produce as much food at low light levels as those of spruce or fir. Therefore, lodgepole pine produces fewer, larger branches that keep the needles in the brightest sun. Also, lodgepole pine is often self-pruning, dropping branches when they no longer receive enough light to produce more food than they consume. Both spruce and fir produce many small branches with numerous needles all the way to the ground, even though such lower branches are shaded. These "inefficient" branches are not shed like those of lodgepole pine. When a lodgepole pine tree dies and falls over, a log lies on the forest floor with a few large branches near the top. When a spruce or fir dies, a great tangle of small branches surrounds the log, providing a good fuel bed.

The number and age of spruce and fir trees in a stand is largely dependent on the age of the forest and the growing conditions of the site. The trees do not become established in large numbers under the lodgepole pines until about 150 years after a fire, and they do not become a significant part of the overstory until about 100 to 150 years later.

Lodgepole pine are commonly thought of as a fire-dependent

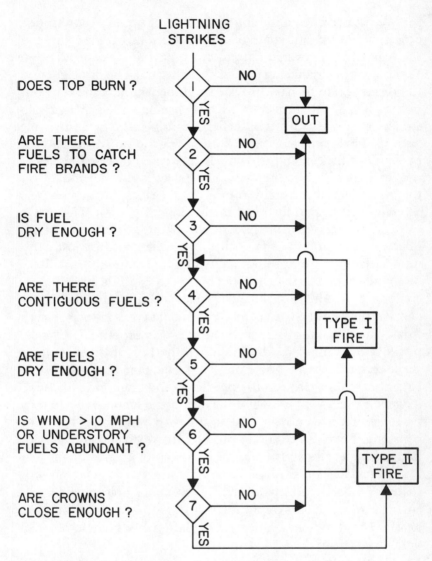

Figure 39. Flow chart for forest fires

Note: Type I fires are those that burn very slowly, usually without burning many tree crowns; type II fires are crown fires that burn all the trees over many acres in a short time.

species because some of the cones require heat to melt a resin between the cone scales before they can open and allow the seed to disperse. This condition, called serotiny, is especially prevalent in areas where fires are quite frequent. Because of this, many people assume that lodgepole pine forests burn more frequently than other forests.

The fires that have been allowed to burn freely in Yellowstone indicate that this is probably not the case here. If fires started and burned in a totally random manner then it would be expected that the number of fire starts and acres burned in a particular vegetation type would be proportionate to the area covered by that vegetation type. These statistics have been compiled in tables 20 and 21 and tested for statistical significance (to see if the differences are likely to be the product of random fluctuations). The vegetation types used were the major cover types or stand-age classes described in detail in Chapter 3.

Fire starts are much more frequent in older classes and much less frequent in younger classes than expected on the basis of random fluctuations (Table 20). The effect of age class is even more pronounced when we consider the number of acres of each cover type burned (Table 21). These statistics indicate that old-growth

TABLE 20
Relationship of fire starts to forest type, 1979–1987

Cover type	Portion of park forest area	No. of fires in type	Expected no. of fires	Chi square
LP0	2.13	1	3	1.2231
LP1	10.19	1	14	11.8256***
LP2	30.24	27	41	4.6810*
LP3	23.97	51	32	10.7401**
SF	5.91	20	8	17.6638***
LP	8.73	7	12	1.9440
DF	6.26	12	8	1.4696
WB	12.49	16	17	0.0446
Total		135	135	

*Asterisks indicate level of statistical significance.

TABLE 21

Acreage of different forest cover types burned in large fires that were allowed to burn naturally, 1972–1986

	COVER TYPE[1]							
Fire name	LP3	WB	LP	SF	LP4/NF[2]	SF/NF	WB/NF	Total area
	OLD GROWTH FORESTS							
Two Ocean	219	683		868				1,770
Forest Lake	3,007	327	222	23	260			3,839
Gallatin	1,876	22		196	110	574		2,778
Washburn	916	18	107				90	1,131
Sulphur/Astringent	1,824		242	517				2,583
Divide/Continental	483			792				1,275
Beaver/Heart/Witch	3,672		213					3,885
Total	11,997	1,050	784	2,396	370	574	90	17,261
Percent of total	55.92%	4.89%	3.65%	11.17%	1.72%	2.68%	0.42%	80.46%
Expected acres	3,855	1,384	1,143	899	131	191	1,000	
Chi-square	17,194	81	113	2,493	437	768	82	
Cole's index of association	0.436	−0.376	−0.847	0.064	0.016	0.018	−0.926	

COVER TYPE[1]

Fire name	LP2	YOUNGER FORESTS			Total area	Grand Total
		LP1	LP0	WB1		
Two Ocean	70			116	186	1,956
Forest Lake	57	734	108		899	4,738
Gallatin	757	41			798	3,576
Washburn	585				585	1,716
Sulphur/Astringent	366	4	28		398	2,981
Divide/Continental	178				178	1,453
Beaver/Heart/Witch	353	638	132	26	1,149	5,034
Total	2,366	1,417	268	142	4,193	21,454
Percent of total	11.03%	6.60%	1.25%	0.66%	19.54%	100.00%
Expected acres	4,746	1,575	326	182		
Chi-square		16	10	9		
Cole's index of association	-0.592	-0.667	-0.324	-0.358		

[1]For cover type descriptions, see Chapter 3.
[2]NF=nonforest.

forests are much more likely to catch fire from a lightning storm and much more likely to burn afterward than are younger stands. Crown fires are largely dependent on the heat produced by burning fuels on the forest floor (12), and the younger forests in Yellowstone do not have much fuel. Large fires typically burn up to younger lodgepole pine forests and either stop or go around them. The young and middle-aged lodgepole pine stands receive a substantial rain of firebrands, which can ignite and burn rotten logs or small pockets of fuel, but there is not enough fuel to cause the crowns to burn to any significant extent. In this way, fires form natural firebreaks that last for 150 to 300 years.

Effects of Smoke

Great quantities of smoke are produced in a fire, especially during and immediately after a run. Very often a temperature inversion develops after the sun goes down. The stable air near the ground is then filled with wood smoke, which has been shown to have antifungal properties (13). This must certainly have some influence on both plant pathogens and decomposer organisms. Apparently, no field work has been done to determine what these effects might be or how long they may last. More research is needed to address the effect of smoke in the total ecosystem.

Smoke becomes a problem in the park only if it obscures highways or blankets a campground or other visitor facility. Occasionally, large quantities of smoke are produced and neighboring communities are affected for a short time. In those instances when the public was contacted before the fire and the program was adequately explained, little concern was expressed when the fire came. However, if the smoke catches a community by surprise, many negative comments are received by park officials.

Effects on Fish and Other Wildlife

Two small watersheds (average late-season flow of about 0.5 cubic feet per second) were burned over in the Divide fire of 1976. These streams had served as spawning areas for native cutthroat trout. Following the fire, eggs in the stream bottoms were examined and found to be viable, and cutthroat trout fry were later observed in the streams. The fire did not kill the eggs nor did it create conditions unfavorable to the survival or growth of the small fish.

Water samples taken from the streams indicated that only during thundershowers and possibly spring snowmelt did water quality in these small streams depart from preburn values. Then, only phosphates were significantly higher. A study was conducted on a nearby watershed that experienced contiguous crown fires in 1931 and 1940 (14). At the time of the study (early 1970s), the sparse tree saplings were 10 to 12 feet tall in the older burn and 6 to 8 feet tall in the younger. It was demonstrated that the burned portion of the stream warmed up earlier in the spring and remained warm longer into the fall. Larger crops of microorganisms and invertebrates resulted. Fish eggs hatched earlier and the fry grew faster and migrated to the lake earlier in the summer as larger fish, giving them a competitive advantage. The removal of the trees that shaded the stream was a benefit to the native fish in that stream. Research is currently under way to determine the effects of the larger 1988 fires on the park's fisheries.

Research was also conducted to determine the immediate effects of crown fire on the bird and small mammal populations (15). The study compared burned areas with adjacent unburned areas. Three successive summers' sampling indicated that the nesting density of 18 species of birds was higher in the burned forest, while that of 12 other species was lower. The fires nearly eliminated habitat for three species, while habitat was greatly enhanced or created for eight species. Two of the species favored by the fire, northern three-toed woodpeckers and mountain bluebirds, are considered rare or declining in population. Fire suppression may be responsible for this status (16).

Trapping for small mammals indicated that, in unburned forests, redbacked voles were more abundant than deer mice. Immediately after the fire and for the first year or two, deer mice were quite abundant while redbacked voles were absent or rare. This relationship returned to near preburn status within three to five years. Redbacked voles feed largely on fungi, while deer mice feed on insects and plant parts. One trapping study initiated six weeks after the 1979 Gallatin fire showed that the redbacked voles were already gone and deer mice had invaded. This relationship held through the next summer. By the second summer, the voles had returned and the deer mice had declined in number (17).

Animal tracks are commonly found in the ashes within a few weeks after a fire. Evidence of ungulate grazing is common and widespread in burned areas the first year postfire. Moose have been commonly sighted by hikers in one of the larger burned areas. Herds of elk and bison are seen feeding in burned areas until canopy closure (when the tree crowns get large enough to touch each other) occurs, 40 to 50 years postfire.

No detailed sampling of insects has yet been done. It has been apparent, however, that much insect activity occurs in the recently killed trees. Pulling back the bark of a large spruce reveals numerous larvae of several species. While fires were still smoking, it was common to see horntailed wasps flying among the freshly killed trees and depositing their eggs. Early spring examination of burned areas reveals evidence of woodpecker feeding on most trees.

Effects on Forest Floor Plants

During the 1979 Gallatin fire, vegetation was sampled in two different communities that were later burned by crown fire. One community was about 190 years old; was dominated by Engelmann spruce, subalpine fir, and lodgepole pine; and was situated in a slight depression providing a moist water regime. Soils were derived from glacial till of andesitic and sedimentary origin. The understory consisted of dense fir reproduction (9,098 stems/acre), and the forest floor was dominated by elk sedge and heartleaf arnica. Fireweed, western meadowrue, a species of aster, and grouse whortleberry also contributed about 1 percent each to the understory. Seven other species were encountered in the sample plots.

The other community was about 280 years old, was dominated by lodgepole pine, and was situated on a level area with a coarse, dry soil derived mainly from rhyolite. The understory was moderately dense with lodgepole pine (1,878 stems/acre), whitebark pine (615 stems/acre), and subalpine fir (453 stems/acre). The forest floor was primarily covered with grouse whortleberry with only minor amounts of four other species. For four consecutive years postfire and again in the sixth and eighth year, the same plots were resampled.

In the spruce-fir stand, after one growing season only half as many species were present. Grouse whortleberry, elk sedge, fireweed, and heartleaf arnica were the only prefire species remaining. Two new species appeared, dandelion and a liverwort. The number of species continued to increase each year, and by the eighth year 20 species were encountered in the sample plots. However, six of the original twelve species had not reappeared. By the eighth year more than a thousand lodgepole pine seedlings per acre occupied the area, and Engelmann spruce and whitebark pine had become established on the plot.

The lodgepole pine stand had only half as many species as the spruce-fir stand before the fire, but after the first growing season it had nearly as many species as it did before the burn. Only heartleaf arnica was common to both species lists. The number of species also continued to increase in this stand, and after eight years there were an equal number of species in both the spruce-fir and the lodgepole pine stands. By the eighth year almost a thousand lodgepole pine seedlings per acre had become established, and a few Engelmann spruce were noticeable.

There were some interesting differences in the behavior of the species in each stand. Only half of the species were common to both stands. Grouse whortleberry covered nearly 60 percent of the preburn lodgepole pine stand but after eight years it was still rare. In the preburn spruce-fir stand, grouse whortleberry covered only 1 percent of the area, but after eight years this had increased to 22 percent cover. In both stands, heartleaf arnica came back strong after the fire and reached a peak in the third year, but after eight years it was almost nonexistent. The sedges increased in cover through the sixth year and then declined slightly by the eighth. They behaved similarly in both stands, but the cover was about twice as high in the lodgepole pine stand. There also was a shift in the relative proportions of elk sedge and Ross's sedge. Elk sedge was most common before the fire and Ross's sedge was most common after the fire.

Regrowth of several species began immediately after the burn. In portions that burned in early July, fireweed was observed to flower and set seed by the end of that growing season. Bluejoint reedgrass immediately began regrowth in moist areas. Most of the plants that were present in both preburn and postburn forests resprouted from plant parts that were present prefire. The sedge in the postfire lodgepole pine stand may have come from seed lying dormant in the soil.

A similar successional pattern was observed after fires that occurred in other areas of the park. Within three to five years, vegetative ground cover is equal to that of nearby unburned stands. Fireweed increases in both frequency and cover for several years. Species continue to increase in cover and frequency until canopy closure, about 40 years postfire (18).

Immediately following a fire, ashes cover the ground surface and form pockets up to four or five inches deep in places. Summer rain showers compact the ashes and start to leach the mineral nutrients back into the soil. The first winter's snow completes the process, and by the first growing season the soils are highly fertile. The plants respond with greatly accelerated growth rates compared to the same species in neighboring unburned stands. Three-year-old lodgepole pine seedlings were observed to have grown to eight inches in height with needles two to three inches long. Lodgepole pine seedlings of the same age in unburned forests are often less than three inches tall with needles about one inch long or less. Fireweed was grazed extensively for several years postfire, and elk sedge, which is seldom grazed in unburned forests, was commonly grazed in burned areas two to five years postfire. These plants were probably grazed more heavily because they had higher nutritive value than plants of the same species from unburned stands, as a result of the ashes.

Crown fire has been a part of the ecosystems of Yellowstone National Park for millennia. Of course, the affected area is drastically altered, but the black trunks, dead trees, and charred forest floor are certainly not devoid of life. A fire creates unique niches that can be utilized by many organisms.

Insects

All plants support a suite of herbivores. Some of these herbivores are large and conspicuous, such as elk, bison, and moose;

others are small, inconspicuous, and most often referred to as pests. We usually try to ignore insects; however, forest insects often become numerous enough to kill many overstory trees, thus changing the density of the larger components of the plant community. Several species of native insects have caused such changes in Yellowstone and they continue to do so.

Spruce budworms have killed numerous trees in Douglas-fir stands of the northern and southwestern parts of the park. This was one of the first insects to cause great concern in Yellowstone. Money was requested from Congress as early as 1924 to provide for control measures for this species. When someone in the office of the Director of the Budget suggested this would be a waste of funds because the epidemic would eventually die out on its own, a high-ranking bureaucrat remarked, "We might just as well watch lightning strike in the Park kindling fires and then sit back content with the feeling that nothing was necessary to be done since they could eventually burn themselves out anyway" (19).

Spruce budworm is still a component of the Douglas-fir communities and still reaches epidemic levels despite the early campaign to eliminate it and a subsequent effort with aerial application of DDT in the 1950s. Even then there were some who wondered if the ecological costs of the spraying were outweighed by the supposed gains.

Mountain pine beetle is another insect that has caused widespread and dramatic mortality in the park's pine species. This beetle is also a member of the native fauna. Pictures taken by some of the earliest visitors to the park show lodgepole pine forests containing numerous dead trees very similar to modern stands that have been under beetle attack for several years. The beetles are evident throughout the park. The population levels, however, are sometimes very low and inconspicuous (endemic levels) and at other times are very high, causing significant mortality over large areas (epidemic levels). The latest outbreak spread into the park about 1969 and lasted until the mid-1980s. It appears that two overlapping outbreaks may have occurred during that time period (Fig. 40).

The first recorded infestation began in the southwest corner of the park in 1930. It spread into the park from adjacent Forest Service lands. This particular cycle had started in Canada several years earlier, spread southward on the west side of the Continental Divide, and then moved east (20).

182

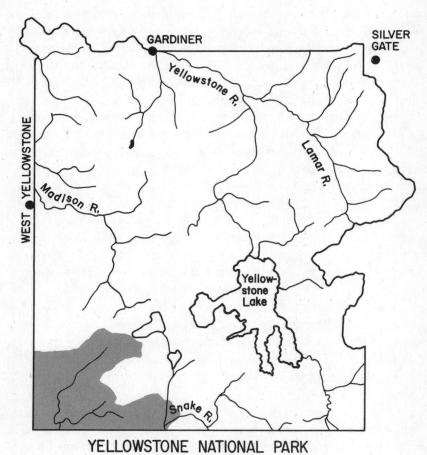

YELLOWSTONE NATIONAL PARK

Figure 40A. Progress of the mountain pine beetle, 1970

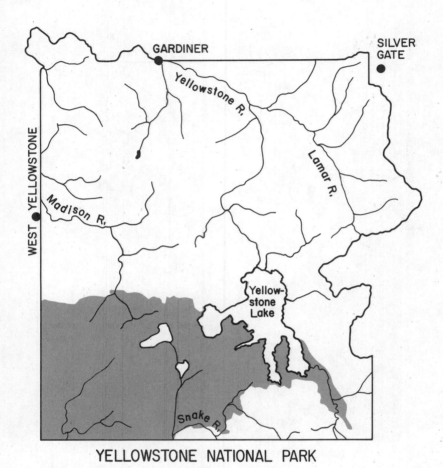

YELLOWSTONE NATIONAL PARK

Figure 40B. Progress of the mountain pine beetle, 1971

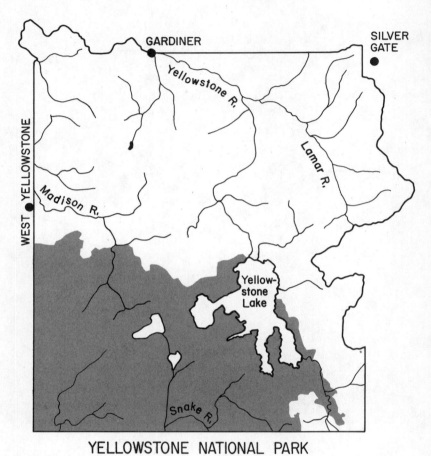

YELLOWSTONE NATIONAL PARK

Figure 40C. Progress of the mountain pine beetle, 1972

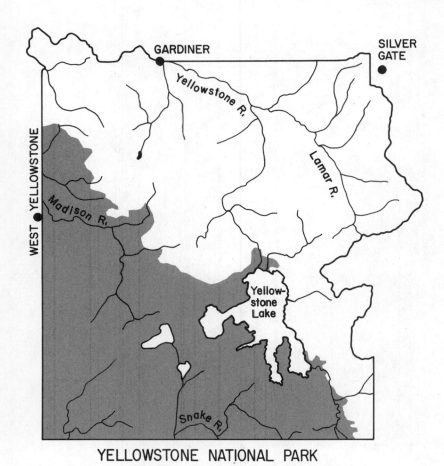

YELLOWSTONE NATIONAL PARK

Figure 40D. Progress of the mountain pine beetle, 1973

186

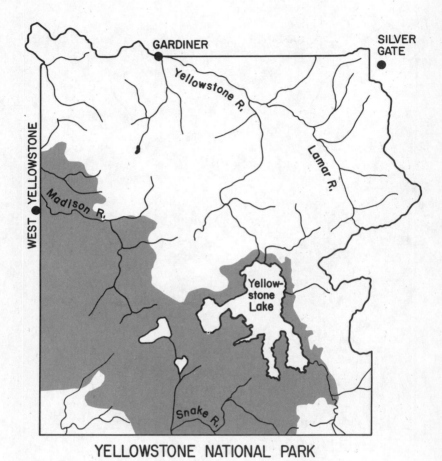

YELLOWSTONE NATIONAL PARK

Figure 40E. Progress of the mountain pine beetle, 1974

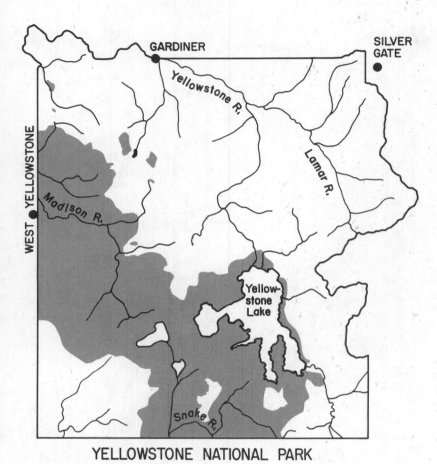

YELLOWSTONE NATIONAL PARK

Figure 40F. Progress of the mountain pine beetle, 1975

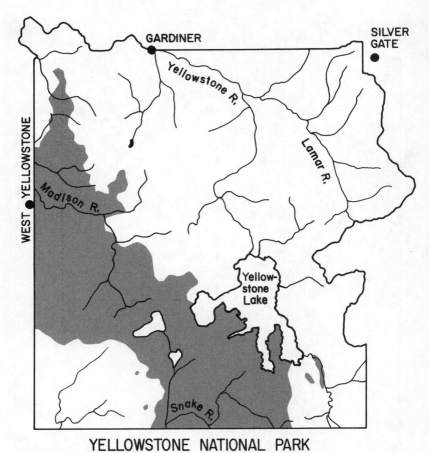

YELLOWSTONE NATIONAL PARK

Figure 40G. Progress of the mountain pine beetle, 1976

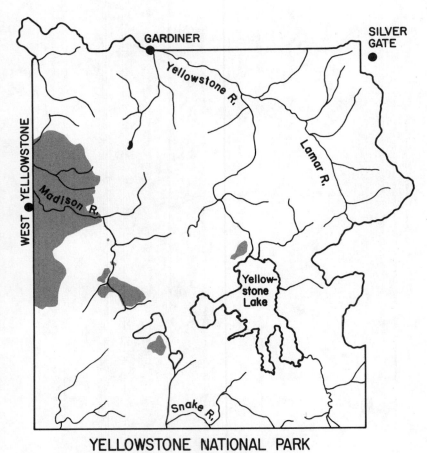

YELLOWSTONE NATIONAL PARK

Figure 40H. Progress of the mountain pine beetle, 1977

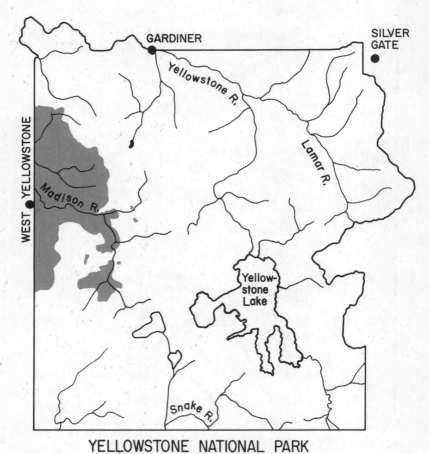

YELLOWSTONE NATIONAL PARK

Figure 40I. Progress of the mountain pine beetle, 1978

191

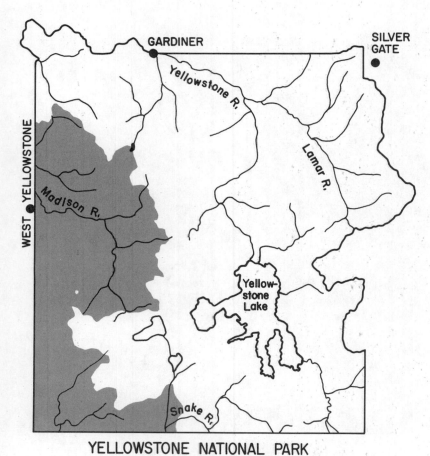

YELLOWSTONE NATIONAL PARK

Figure 40J. Progress of the mountain pine beetle, 1979

192

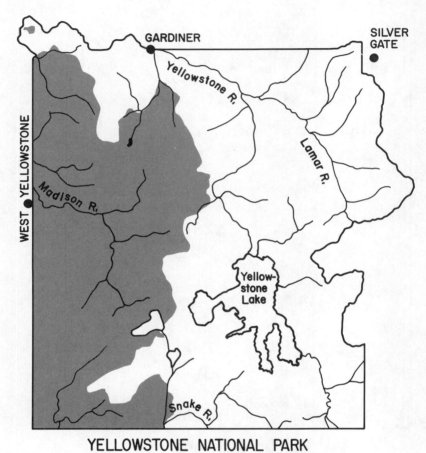

YELLOWSTONE NATIONAL PARK

Figure 40K. Progress of the mountain pine beetle, 1980

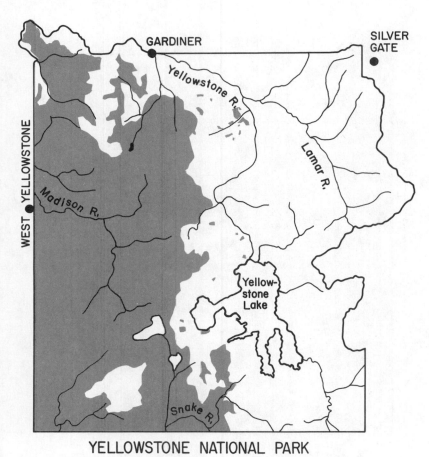

YELLOWSTONE NATIONAL PARK

Figure 40L. Progress of the mountain pine beetle, 1981

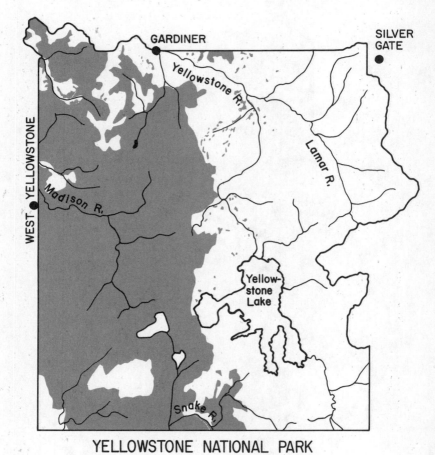

YELLOWSTONE NATIONAL PARK

Figure 40M. Progress of the mountain pine beetle, 1982

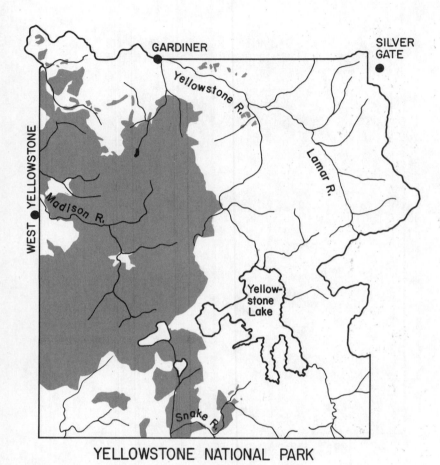

YELLOWSTONE NATIONAL PARK

Figure 40N. Progress of the mountain pine beetle, 1983

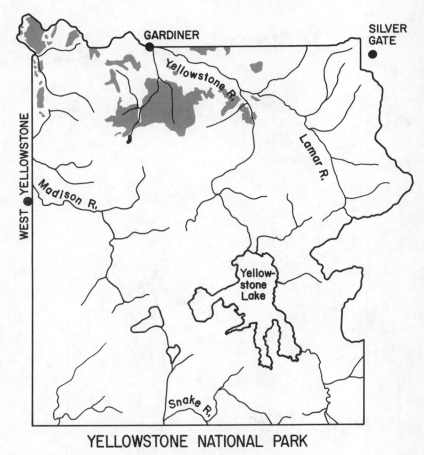

YELLOWSTONE NATIONAL PARK

Figure 40O. Progress of the mountain pine beetle, 1984

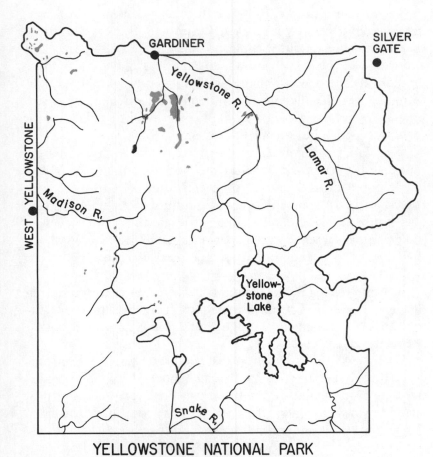

YELLOWSTONE NATIONAL PARK
Figure 40P. Progress of the mountain pine beetle, 1985

Control measures (cutting and burning or burning the standing, infected trees) were immediately instituted. Surveys were made to ascertain the extent of the problem, but by 1934 the spread and extent of the infestation was so large that all hope was abandoned and control was limited to the campgrounds and roadsides. Comments by the investigators of the time indicate that whitebark pines were hardest hit and lodgepole pines only sustained minor losses except in the southwest corner.

By 1937, the survey showed that practically all the whitebark pine stands in the park were heavily infested. The next year, the beetle populations appeared to be decreasing. Control was continued in the Mammoth Campground until 1939. In 1940, the beetles were not considered to be a serious problem, but they were still present at epidemic levels parkwide in whitebark pine. By 1942, they were no longer considered a serious problem even in whitebark pine.

It is interesting to note that both outbreaks occurred during droughts and ended during wet periods. Total precipitation during the 1980s has not been high, but summer precipitation has been well above normal.

There has been speculation that the beetles cause a drastic increase in fuels, setting the stage for large, intense fires. This speculation has been offered so often that it is now accepted as proven fact. However, for more than 50 years the southwest corner of the park has been under nearly continuous beetle attack with only a few years between waves. The vegetation has still not been converted to another timber type, and large fires are no more frequent there than in other parts of the park. In fact, since the institution of Yellowstone's natural fire program in 1972, several fires have started in that corner. All were allowed to burn themselves out, but none of these fires became as spectacular as the fires that occurred in areas that sustained lighter beetle damage or that had not been infested within the last 50+ years.

There probably is an interaction between mountain pine beetles and fire, but it may be just the opposite of that expected. Fuels suitable for crown fires may be reduced by the beetles to the point of retarding fires.

Before I explain my reasoning behind this theory, an explanation of fire as it relates to fuel may be helpful. Live plants can contain more than twice as much water as burnable material. This moisture must all be evaporated before the fuel can burn. Fires just do not produce enough heat to dry out and consume live fuels larger than about ¼-inch in diameter. Dead fuels of larger diameter are consumed, but even in the hottest fires, only the outer inch or less of the trunks burn. After the fire front passes, fire continues to burn in those places where fallen trunks cross. It is common to see the ends of four or six blackened logs radiating from a common point, reminiscent of a giant campfire that did not burn well.

Beetles, of course, do not consume the trunks. They eat the inner bark and thereby kill the trees. The needles dry out and turn red. But even during a severe attack, less than 30 percent of the standing trees are killed in any one year (21). In one study conducted in the southwest corner of the park, the greatest number of trees killed in one year was only 13 percent of the living trees (22). Reports of large increases in fuel load following a beetle attack do not point out that the increases are all in the dead-and-down category nor that most of the increase is in the larger-than-three-inch size class. During the time when the needles are dead and still on the tree (approximately one year), fires may be able to burn slightly better in the stand than they would if all the needles were green. But as the needles fall off the trees and become incorporated in the duff of the forest floor, the fuel available to a crown fire actually decreases. This decrease continues as long as the beetle attack continues.

The dead-and-down trunks may make firefighting extremely difficult and may contribute to a slightly higher heat release over a longer time period, as the outer layers of wood burn and those isolated pockets where the trunks are stacked just right are consumed. There may be some slight effect on the early stages of plant succession resulting from a larger heat pulse entering the soil and killing more of the plants, but the extent or size of a fire is not greatly increased by the effects of beetle kill.

As I write this (October 1987), a fire is burning near the South Entrance in an area that was attacked severely by beetles in the mid-1960s and again in the mid-1970s. The fire started six weeks ago and has attained the size of 130 acres. The weather has been dry and strong winds have blown on several occasions. If the tree crowns had not been killed by beetles the fire probably would have burned several hundred to several thousand acres. (As I rewrite, the fire season has drawn to a close and the accuracy of my prediction can be assessed. The fire reached 943 acres [23]. Much of the spread was in the lodgepole pine reproduction, and some of my colleagues maintain that the lodgepole pine reproduction was more dense because of the sparse overstory created by the beetles. So goes the never-ending search for "truth" known as research. More plots will be examined in the summer of 1990 and more hypotheses will be put forward.)

There is a beetle-fire interaction in the suitability of the trees as a food source. The beetles have evolved a life strategy of selecting large, apparently healthy trees in which to lay their eggs (24). They have not however, evolved highly successful search strategies and are thus dependent on great numbers of large trees near one another to irrupt. Pine trees that grow up after a fire will be too small for beetle attack for a long period. In severe beetle attack areas, green islands of younger trees are scattered throughout the sea of temporarily red-topped older forests. As these stands mature, large areas of trees become suitable feeding and egg-laying sites simultaneously; the beetles enjoy a feast.

Studies have shown that nutrients released by the decay of the dead trees or those made available because of the death of a competitor are quickly taken up by the plant community and rapidly utilized in increased growth (25). However, because of the cool dry climate of Yellowstone, this does not cause a great increase in fuels available to fires.

There is much yet to be learned about and from the mountain pine beetle. Succession following disturbance by mountain pine beetle is also different from that following fire. All the large trees are not killed by the beetle. Representatives of trees in all the size classes are left. Most of the trees larger than 12 inches dbh are killed, but in the 4-inch-and-less size class most of the trees survive (21). The surviving forest is often a strange-appearing stand of trees with a few large, old lodgepole pine monarchs standing above a ragged, partly even-aged stand of younger trees. The younger trees are mostly lodgepole pine, but Engelmann spruce and subalpine fir may also be common depending on the site conditions and the age of the stand attacked. The forest floor plants are affected little except that they are slightly more vigorous, owing to the increased sunlight and available nutrients no longer taken up by the larger trees.

Wind

Wind also can be a powerful force in a forested community. The large woody stems of trees give them an advantage over the herbaceous plants and shrubs in the competition for light, but this advantage comes at the cost of increased vulnerability to windthrow. Each year another increment of wood is created, and the tree crown gets larger and more susceptible to extreme winds. In the economics of life, it is not feasible to prepare for the extremes of environmental conditions. Too many resources would be spent on providing contingencies for rare events.

Tornadoes, of course, produce extreme winds sufficient to blow over or break off all the large trees in a stand. Occasional severe downdrafts from thunderstorms do the same thing, and blowdowns, as they are called, are evident in the park in a few places. Recent blowdowns can be distinguished from recent fires because the downed trunks are all pointing in the direction the wind blew. In 1984, a severe wind event skipped across the park leaving behind a series of blowdowns ranging from 1 to 100 acres, blowing trees over on a total of 660 acres. Another blowdown of 750 acres occurred in the 1970s along the western boundary.

Evidence of blowdowns is not as long-lasting as evidence of fires. As soon as the crowns of surviving younger trees have completely recovered the site, the distinguishing tree orientation is no longer visible from the air, and as the fallen trunks decompose all evidence of the blowdown is obliterated. Some patches of younger trees that are thought to be evidence of past fires may actually indicate blowdowns.

Succession following a blowdown is different from that following a fire. The plant community does not start from the same point. For the most part, a blowdown does not disturb the plants of the

TABLE 22
Tree reproduction in a blowdown and in the neighboring forest after three growing seasons*

Site No.	Position	Lodgepole Pine		Whitebark Pine		Subalpine Fir		Engelmann Spruce	
		Pre-	Post-	Pre-	Post-	Pre-	Post-	Pre-	Post-
1	Inside	134 (44)	100 (46)	9 (6)	0	0.4 (.02)	1 (1)	0	0.2 (0.2)
	Outside	88 (23)	128 (80)	13 (5)	0	0.4 (0.2)	0	0	0
2	Inside	39 (9)	17 (6)	5 (2)	0	0	0	0	0
	Outside	68 (16)	31 (12)	5 (2)	0	0.2 (.02)	0	0	0

Plot size is 50 square meters.
Numbers in parentheses are standard error of mean.
*Reproduction was classed as pre- or postdisturbance.

forest floor except where the root balls of the trees are forced out of the ground. Smaller trees are not eliminated, and the next genera-tion of overstory trees does not need to pass through the exigen-cies of competing with the herbaceous plants. Following a fire, lodgepole pine are clearly dominant in the succeeding forest, but in a blowdown, the spruce and fir trees that were previously estab-lished under the overstory are able to continue growth and com-pete well with the lodgepole pine.

Tree reproduction was measured in a three-year-old blowdown. Two sites were chosen: one in a moderately dry area where the original forest was about 270 years old and another in a very dry area where the original forest was about 330 years old (Table 22). Spruce and fir seedlings were few, suggesting that both moisture condition and mineral nutrition are poor on both sites. The moister of the two stands had more seedlings and more species than the drier stand. The young trees in both places that were older than the blowdown ranged in size from tiny seedlings that appeared to be four to ten years in age to small trees of three to four inches dbh.

The removal of the overstory had surprisingly little effect on either the number or size of the seedlings. There was no significant difference in the number of new seedlings in the blowdown and in the neighboring intact stands. The post-blowdown seedlings were much smaller than those of the same age found in burned forests, and the herbaceous plants were not growing luxuriantly the way they do after a fire. Minerals that would have been available from the ash of a fire were conspicuously lacking. As forests develop at both sites they will be dominated by lodgepole pine, but the age structure will be somewhat more variable than following fire and the moist area may have a few more spruce and fir.

PART THREE
Using Vegetation Information

Vegetation and Management

8

The National Park Service is mandated to preserve Yellowstone in as natural a state as possible, which requires that managers consider a number of complex environmental factors when land management actions are needed. Vegetation data can be useful to those who must manipulate or protect natural landscapes. A large number of factors determine the growing conditions of any site and thus the biotic community present and the response of that community to disturbance. Some of these factors are easily measured; some are measured with difficulty; and some can only be measured indirectly. We may not recognize the existence of still others. Thus, direct measurement of all factors on a site is impractical at best, if not impossible. Plants, on the other hand, are easily observed, and because they integrate all the factors influencing a site they may be used as indicators of the sum of all environmental factors and the interactions among those factors.

Inferences about a site's potential or its ability to produce certain plant combinations, as well as its biomass production potential, can be made if the habitat type to which it belongs is known. Efforts to relate site potential to parameters of interest to managers have already been made to describe the potential of logging sites for tree reproduction (1), the amount of lumber expected from a timber sale (2), and the distribution of bird species (3). However, the successional stage of the plant community is also extremely important because the characteristics of the seral communities can be quite different from those of the climax community. The position of a site in both the habitat type and cover type system is important in determining the characteristics of a site. Characteristics of an LP3 cover type on a subalpine fir/grouse whortleberry habitat

type are different from those of an LP3 cover type on a subalpine
fir/globe huckleberry habitat type. The dual classification described
here has several advantages when it comes to making inferences
about site conditions. The physical environment is indicated by
habitat type and the ramifications of succession are indicated by
cover type.

The habitat types and cover types of the landscape can be
mapped and the geographical relationships of the various pieces
determined. Within the limits of precision of both the classification and the mapping effort, the potential of a very large area can
be ascertained.

The vegetation data gathered so far in Yellowstone have already
been put to use in several instances. Perhaps the most extensive
is the assessment of grizzly bear habitat. The following paragraphs
outline some of the ways vegetation data have been used or may
be used in the future.

Assessment of Animal Habitats

Animals obtain their food and cover from plants both directly
and indirectly. For this reason, plant communities are a significant
variable in the equation of survival of an animal population. Some
plant communities have abundant animal foods and others very
little. The ability to stratify this heterogeneity is necessary before
an assessment can be made of the effects of human activities on
the animal's environment. The habitat type/cover type system provides such a stratification tool (4).

An example of the use of this tool is the Cumulative Effects
model for grizzly bears in the greater Yellowstone ecosystem (5).
This model is used to assess the impact of human activity on grizzly
bear habitat in Yellowstone and the surrounding areas occupied
by grizzly bears. It is based on mapped data manipulated by computer (people working with this sort of thing call it a geographic
information system, or GIS).

A habitat index value was determined for each habitat type/
cover type combination (plant community type), and an estimated
displacement coefficient and zone of influence were assigned to
each class of human activity. Areas of concentrated animal foods

(such as fish-spawning streams and winter ranges where winter-killed animals are abundant) were mapped and incorporated into the habitat index value. The total value of an area is obtained by multiplying the acres of each plant community type by its habitat index value to obtain the number of habitat units in the area. Habitat units are the unit of exchange for this process, much like money is the unit of exchange for our economic system.

The computer then overlays the various maps and discounts the value of the area within the zones of influence by the displacement coefficient. For example, if only half of the elk carcasses within a mile of a road were used by grizzly bears, all the areas within a mile of the road would have half the value of the same type of area outside this zone of influence. In this way, the amount of habitat taken from the grizzly bear by our activities can be assessed in terms of habitat units and the cumulative effects of all our present activities and any planned activities can be approximated. With this tool, land managers both within and outside the park can better evaluate the effects of their management decisions on the grizzly bear and perhaps mitigate for loss of habitat or even forgo some activities in order to ensure the existence of this magnificent animal.

The examination of the distribution and variation of habitat units has been used to explain some grizzly bear ecology as well. Concentrations of bears can be explained by concentrations of habitat units and bear movement can be related to changes in these concentrations by seasons. Variation from year to year in the value of these units can explain the number of human/bear encounters. During years of low value the bears seem to wander around more looking for food in other places and get into trouble more often. This same process can be applied to other animal species if the appropriate studies are conducted to determine the value of the various plant community types to that particular species.

Mountain pine beetles are a common insect in Yellowstone. It is known that these beetles attack trees with the greatest food resources. Trees with the most available food are those growing on good sites that have reached a certain critical diameter. This is precisely the information contained in a habitat type and cover type classification. The extent and intensity of a pine beetle epidemic could be assessed in advance by using the information contained in a vegetation map.

Assessment of Fire Behavior

When an agency makes the decision to allow a forest fire to burn unhindered it assumes a responsibility. Visitor safety and the protection of developments and neighboring lands must be assured. Fire is a natural part of the Yellowstone environment, and as such it should be allowed to play its natural role.

In carrying out this policy, it is necessary to predict fairly accurately the location and potential maximum extent of a fire. Because of the longevity of many fires, such predictions must forecast condition up to three months in advance. Knowledge of weather has not yet reached a state that allows such long-range forecasting. However, the relationship of a fire to its fuel load does allow us to make an estimate of maximum extent. Cover type has provided a good estimator of fuel load. The location of a fire start in relation to the surrounding cover types can provide a good indication of whether a fire will become very large and how far it might burn. Even if the weather is right for burning, a fire will not burn well in young or middle-aged lodgepole pine.

When a lightning-caused fire is reported in Yellowstone, general fuel moisture conditions are first assessed. If fuels are fairly wet, little action is initiated apart from keeping track of any continued activity of the fire. When fuel moisture is low, the exact location of the fire and its relationship to the various cover types is determined. A tentative prediction of the probable maximum extent of the fire is made, and a decision is reached whether or not the fire should be extinguished. As the fire progresses, the prediction is constantly reassessed. Experience so far has shown that cover type is a good predictor of both fire behavior and extent.

Assessment of Revegetation Needs

A third application for vegetation information is in the revegetation of ground disturbed by construction. Disturbances associated with human occupation are a frequent and continuing occurrence, albeit comparatively minimal in the park. Utility lines are emplaced, repaired, and moved; roads are built and realigned; and buildings are erected, moved, and replaced. All these activities leave behind bare ground. In Yellowstone, the most desirable vegetation should be that which would occur on the site if it had not been disturbed. Knowledge of the various plant communities and their environmental limits would aid in determining which plant species to put back on the site. Knowledge of the predisturbance vegetation should act as a guide to what would do best on the site.

A basic knowledge of vegetation not only has great utilitarian value in how we manipulate our environment, but it has esthetic value as well. As we observe our surroundings our appreciation for what we see is in direct proportion to how much we know about the things we see. If we see a only monotonous blanket of trees and grass, we miss so much of what is available to enjoy.

References and Notes

Introduction

1. R. Daubenmire. 1952. "Forest vegetation of northern Idaho and adjacent Washington, and its bearing on concepts of vegetation classification." *Ecological Monographs* 22:301–330.
2. R.D. Pfister, B.L. Kovalchik, S.F. Arno, and R.C. Presby. 1977. *Forest habitat types of Montana*. General Technical Report INT-34. U.S.D.A., Forest Service, Intermountain Forest and Range Experiment Station. 174 pp.; W.F. Mueggler and W.L. Stewart. 1980. *Grassland and shrubland habitat types of Montana*. General Technical Report INT-66. U.S.D.A., Forest Service, Intermountain Forest and Range Experiment Station. 154 pp.; M. Hironaka, M.A. Fosberg, and A.H. Winward. 1983. *Sagebrush-grass habitat types of southern Idaho*. Bull. No. 35. University of Idaho, Moscow, Forest, Wildlife, and Range Experiment Station. 44 pp.; D.J. Mattson. 1984. "Classification and environmental relationships of wetland vegetation in central Yellowstone National Park." M.S. thesis. University of Idaho, Moscow. 409 pp.
3. The term *habitat type* is often confused with the term *climax community*, the potential vegetation of a site. This is an easy trap to fall into because of the use of plant names to designate a type. The original publication of the concept, however, quite specifically indicates that the environment and not the plant community is being classified. The plants are used only as a convenient indicator of the environment. The particular physical attribute that distinguishes a type could be used as a designator, but that can be very difficult to determine.
4. D.G. Despain. 1977. "Forest successional stages in Yellowstone National Park." Information Paper No. 32. Yellowstone National Park. 3 pp.

Chapter 1

1. D.B. Houston. 1973. "Wild fires in Yellowstone National Park." *Ecology* 54:1111–1117.
2. D.J. Mattson. 1984. "Classification and environmental relationships of wetland vegetation in central Yellowstone National Park." M.S. thesis. University of Idaho, Moscow. 409 pp.

3. B.V. Barnes. 1975. "Phenotypic variation of trembling aspen of western North America." *Forest Science* 21:319–328.
4. A. Chase. 1986. *Playing God in Yellowstone,* p. 115. New York: Atlantic Monthly Press. 446 pp.
5. N.V. DeByle. 1979. "Potential effects of stable versus fluctuating elk populations in the aspen ecosystem," pp. 13–19. In M.S. Boyce and L.D. Hayden-Wing, eds. *North American elk, ecology, behavior and management,* conference proceedings. University of Wyoming, Laramie, April 3–5, 1978.

Chapter 2

1. J.S. Sheppard. 1971. "The influence of geothermal temperature gradients upon vegetation patterns in Yellowstone National Park." Ph.D. thesis. Colorado State University, Ft. Collins. 159 pp.

Chapter 4

1. E.B. Leopold and H.D. MacGinite. 1972. "Development and affinities of Tertiary floras in the Rocky Mountains," pp. 147–200. In A. Grahm, ed. *Floristics and paleofloristics of Asia and eastern North America.* Amsterdam, London, New York: Elsevier Publishing.
2. J.D. Love. 1960. "Cenozoic sedimentation and crustal movement in Wyoming." *American Journal of Science,* Bradley Volume 258-A:204–214.
3. L.W. Alvarez, W. Alvarez, F. Asaro, and H.V. Michel. 1980. "Extraterrestrial cause for the Cretaceous-Tertiary extinction." *Science* 208:1095–1108.
4. R.H. Tschudy, C.L. Pillmore, C.J. Orth, J.S. Gilmore, and J.D. Knight. 1984. "Disruption of the terrestrial plant ecosystem at the Cretaceous-Tertiary boundary, western interior." *Science* 225:1030–1032.
5. J.A. Wolfe. 1978. "A paleological interpretation of Tertiary climates in the Northern Hemisphere." *American Scientist* 66:694–703; C. Chevelier, J.J. Chateauneuf, C. Pomerol, D. Rabussier, M. Renard, and C. Vergnaud-Grazzini. 1981. "The geological events at the Eocene/Oligocene boundary." *Paleogeography, Paleoclimatology, Paleoecology* 36:223–248.
6. J.A. O'Keefe. 1980. "The terminal Eocene event: Formation of a ring system around the earth." *Nature* 285(5763):309–311.
7. E. Dorf. 1942. "Upper Cretaceous floras of the Rocky Mountain region II: Flora of the Lance Formation at the type locality, Niobrara County, Wyoming," pp. 79–159. Pub. No. 508. Carnegie Institution of Washington.
8. J.D. Love and W.R. Keefer. 1975. *Geology of sedimentary rocks in southern Yellowstone National Park.* Professional Paper 729-D. U.S. Geological Survey. 60 pp.
9. T.H. Nilsen and E.H. McKee. 1979. "Paleogeography of the western United States," pp. 257–276. In J.M. Armentrout, M.R. Cole, and H.T. Best, Jr., eds. *Cenozoic paleography of the western United States.* Pacific Coast Paleography Symposium 3, Anaheim, California. Pacific Section of Economic Paleontologists and Mineralogists.
10. E. Dorf. 1960. "Tertiary fossil forests of Yellowstone National Park, Wyoming," pp. 253–260. In D.E. Campau and H.W. Anisgard, eds. Billings

Geological Society 11th annual field conference, conference proceedings. West Yellowstone, September 1960; L.H. Fisk. 1976. "Palynology of the Amethyst Mountain 'Fossil Forest,' Yellowstone National Park, Wyoming." Ph.D. thesis. Loma Linda University, Loma Linda, California. 340 pp.; W. Fritz. 1980. "Reinterpretation of depositional environment of the Yellowstone 'fossil forests.'" *Geology* 8:309–313.

11. J.A. Wolf. 1979. *Temperature parameters of humid to mesic forests of eastern Asia and relation to forests of other regions of the Northern Hemisphere and Australasia.* Professional Paper 1106. U.S. Geological Survey. 37 pp.

12. H.F. Becker. 1961. *Oligocene plants from the upper Ruby River Basin, southwestern Montana.* Memoir 82. Geological Society of America. 127 pp.

13. J.D. Love, M.C. McKenna, and M.R. Dawson. 1976. *Eocene, Oligocene and Miocene rocks and vertebrate fossils at the Emerald Lake locality, 3 miles south of Yellowstone National Park, Wyoming.* Professional Paper 932-A. U.S. Geological Survey. 28 pp.

14. G.M. Richmond, W. Mullenders, and M. Coremans. 1978. "Climatic implications of two pollen analyses from newly recognized rocks of latest Pliocene age in the Washburn Range, Yellowstone National Park, Wyoming." Bulletin 1455. U.S. Geological Survey. 13 pp.; C.W. Barnosky. 1984. "Late Miocene vegetational and climatic variations inferred from a pollen record in northwest Wyoming." *Science* 223:49–51.

15. G.M. Richmond. 1986. "Stratigraphy and chronology of glaciations in Yellowstone National Park, Wyoming," pp. 83–98. In G.M. Richmond and D.S. Fullerton, eds. *Quaternary glaciations in the United States of America. Part II: Quaternary glaciations in the Northern Hemisphere.* London: Pergamon Press; K.L. Pierce. 1979. *History and dynamics of glaciation in the northern Yellowstone National Park area.* Professional Paper 729-F. U.S. Geological Survey. 90 pp.

16. R.G. Baker. 1986. "Sangamonian(?) and Wisconsinan paleoenvironments in Yellowstone National Park." *Geological Society of America Bulletin* 97:717–736.

17. R.G. Baker. 1976. *Late Quaternary vegetation history of the Yellowstone Lake basin, Wyoming.* Professional Paper 729-E. U.S. Geological Survey. 48 pp.

18. A.V. Douglas and C.W. Stockton. 1975. *Long-term reconstruction of seasonal temperature and precipitation in the Yellowstone National Park region using dendroclimatic techniques.* University of Arizona, Tucson, Laboratory of Tree-Ring Research. 86 pp.

Chapter 5

1. F.S. Baker. 1944. "Mountain climates of the western United States." *Ecological Monographs* 14:223–254; G.T. Trewartha. 1961. *The earth's problem climates.* Madison: University of Wisconsin Press. 334 pp.

2. Soil Conservation Service. 1988. *Snow survey and water supply products reference.* Portland, Oregon: Soil Conservation Service, West National Technical Center, Snow Survey Program, Water Supply Forecast Staff, Data Analysis Group. 289 pp.

3. Regression lines for each group of stations shown in Figure 2 are as follows: For the west-side stations WC1 = −95.7 + 0.017(ELEV) r^2 = 0.63 and for the east-side stations WC1 = −82.2 + 0.013(ELEV) r^2 = 0.87, where WC1 = snow-course water content on April 1 and ELEV = elevation in feet. A multiple regression of water content against elevation in feet and distance from the crest in miles accounted for 68 percent of the variation and both independent variables had highly significant regressions [WC1 = −91.2 + .016(ELEV) + 0.27(DIST)].

4. R.A. Dirks and B.E. Martner. 1982. "The climate of Yellowstone and Grand Teton national parks." National Park Service Occasional Paper Number Six. U.S.D.I., National Park Service. 26 pp.

5. R.A. Bryson and F.K. Hare. 1974. "The climates of North America," pp. 1–47. In H.E. Landsberg, ed. *World survey of climatology* vol. 2. Amsterdam, London, New York: Elsevier Scientific Publishing.

6. H. Walter. 1973. *Vegetation of the earth in relation to climate and the eco-physiological conditions*. New York: Springer Verlag. 237 pp.

7. T. Weaver. 1980. "Climates of vegetation types of the northern Rocky mountains and adjacent plains." *American Midland Naturalist* 103:392–398.

8. R.G. Baker. 1976. *Late Quaternary vegetation history of the Yellowstone Lake basin, Wyoming*. Professional Paper 729-E. U.S. Geological Survey. 48 pp.

9. A.V. Douglas and C.W. Stockton. 1975. *Long-term reconstruction of seasonal temperature and precipitation in the Yellowstone National Park region using dendroclimatic techniques*. University of Arizona, Tucson, Laboratory of Tree-Ring Research. 86 pp.

10. W.R. Keefer. 1971. "The geologic story of Yellowstone National Park." Bulletin 1347. U.S. Geological Survey. 92 pp.; U.S. Geological Survey. 1972. *Geologic map of Yellowstone National Park*. Map I-711. U.S. Geological Survey.

11. A.D. Howard, J.W. Williams, and I. Raisz. 1972. "Physiography," pp. 29–31. In W.W. Mallory, ed. *Geologic atlas of the Rocky Mountain region*. Denver, Colorado: Rocky Mountain Association of Geologists.

12. C.C. Trettin. 1986. *Characterization of soils in Yellowstone National Park*. Final Project Report, Contract No. CX-1200-1-B027. L'Anse: Michigan Technological University, Ford Forestry Center.

13. Occasional roots were reported in deeper horizons but all pits did not go below the last roots. In order to standardize the depth across all pits and to account for the most important layers, the described convention was followed.

14. L.C. Cole. 1949. "The measurement of interspecific association." *Ecology* 30:411–424. Cole's index of association was used here because it gives a linear index from −1 to +1.

Chapter 7

1. D.G. Despain. 1983. "Nonpyrogenous climax lodgepole pine communities in Yellowstone National Park." *Ecology* 64:231–234.

2. R.G. Baker. 1976. *Late Quaternary vegetation history of the Yellowstone Lake basin, Wyoming.* Professional Paper 729-E. U.S. Geological Survey. 48 pp.
3. Natural fire is here defined as fire burning without the influence of modern man. Some people prefer the term *prescribed natural fire,* but I would rather use prescribed fire to designate fires that are totally under the control of well-meaning managers. *Wildfire* would be a better term for these fires, showing a relationship to wildlife, but fire suppression officials use that word to identify fires that are unwanted and need suppression.
4. R.E. Sellers and D.G. Despain. 1976. "Fire management in Yellowstone National Park," pp. 99–113. In R. Komarek, ed. *Proceedings.* Tall Timbers Fire Ecology Conference and Intermountain Fire Research Council Fire and Land Management Symposium. Missoula, Montana, October 1974. Tallahassee, Florida: Tall Timbers Research Station.
5. B.E. Martner. 1976. *Drought index and winter severity index for Yellowstone National Park.* University of Wyoming, Laramie, Department of Atmospheric Science. 53 pp.
6. R.A. Dirks and B.E. Martner. 1982. "The climate of Yellowstone and Grand Teton national parks." National Park Service Occasional Paper Number Six. U.S.D.I., National Park Service. 26 pp.
7. D.W. Wear. 1885. *Report of the Superintendent of Yellowstone National Park to the Secretary of the Interior 1885.* Washington, D.C.: Government Printing Office. 5 pp.
8. A.L. Haines. 1977. *The Yellowstone story, a history of our first national park* vol. 1. Yellowstone Library and Museum Association and Colorado Associated University Press. 385 pp.
9. M. Harris. 1886. *Report of the Superintendent of Yellowstone National Park to the Secretary of the Interior 1886.* Washington, D.C.: Government Printing Office. 13 pp.
10. W.H. Romme. 1982. "Fire and landscape diversity in subalpine forests of Yellowstone National Park." *Ecological Monographs* 52:199–221.
11. F.E. Clements. 1910. "The life history of lodgepole pine burn forests." Bulletin 79. U.S.D.A., U.S. Forest Service. 56 pp.
12. C.E. Van Wagner. 1977. "Conditions for the start and spread of crown fire." *Canadian Journal of Forest Research* 7:23–24.
13. J.R. Parmeter, Jr., and Bjarne Uhrenholdt. 1976. "Effects of smoke on pathogens and other fungi," pp. 299–304. In R. Komarek, ed. *Proceedings.* Tall Timbers Fire Ecology Conference and Intermountain Fire Research Council Fire and Land Management Symposium. Missoula, Montana, October 1974. Tallahassee, Florida: Tall Timbers Research Station.
14. D.P. Albin. 1978. "Some effects of forest fires on selected streams in Yellowstone National Park." M.S. thesis. Humbolt State University, Arcata, California. 55 pp.
15. S. Gniadek. 1977. "Some aspects of avian ecology following the 1974 Trail Creek and 1976 Divide fires in Yellowstone National Park." Unpublished

report. On file at Yellowstone National Park. 74 pp.; A.R. Pfister. 1980. "Postfire avian ecology in Yellowstone National Park." M.S. thesis. Washington State University, Pullman. 235 pp.; M.A. Wood. 1981. "Small mammal communities after two recent fires in Yellowstone National Park." M.S. thesis. Montana State University, Bozeman. 58 pp.

16. D.L. Taylor. 1979. "Forest fires and the tree-hole nesting cycle in Grand Teton and Yellowstone national parks," pp. 509–512. In R.M. Linn, ed. *Proceedings of the First Conference on Scientific Research in National Parks.* New Orleans, Louisiana, November 1976. Transactions and Proceedings Series No. 5. U.S.D.I., National Park Service.

17. Personal communication with Jeffrey Alley, October 1982.

18. D.L. Taylor. 1973. "Some ecological implications of forest fire control in Yellowstone National Park, Wyoming." *Ecology* 54:1394–1396.

19. A.B. Cammerer, assistant director of National Park Service. October 28, 1924. Letter to Horace M. Albright, superintendent of Yellowstone National Park. On file at Yellowstone National Park Archives, Wyoming.

20. [Yellowstone] *Superintendent's Annual Report,* 1930 through 1942.

21. W.E. Cole and G.D. Amman. 1980. *Mountain pine beetle dynamics in lodgepole pine forests. Part I: Course of an infestation.* General Technical Report INT-89. U.S.D.A., Forest Service. 56 pp.

22. W.H. Kline, D.L. Parker, and C.E. Jensen. 1978. "Attack, emergence, and stand depletion trends of the mountain pine beetle in a lodgepole pine stand during an outbreak." *Journal of Environmental Entomology* 7:732–737.

23. The fire started on August 8 and lasted until the snow came in mid-November. There was no precipitation for all of October and the first week of November.

24. W.E. Cole and G.D. Amman. 1983. *Mountain pine beetle dynamics in lodgepole pine forests. Part II: Population dynamics.* General Technical Report INT-145. U.S.D.A., Forest Service, Forest and Range Experiment Station. 59 pp.

25. W.H. Romme, D.H. Knight, and J.B. Yavitt. 1986. "Mountain pine beetle outbreaks in the Rocky Mountains: Regulators of primary productivity?" *The American Naturalist* 127:484–494.

Part 3

1. R.D. Pfister. 1972. "Habitat types and regeneration," pp. 120–125. In *Permanent Association Committees Proceedings.* Portland, Oregon: Western Forestry Association.

2. A.R. Stage. 1973. *Prognosis model for stand development.* Research Paper INT-137. U.S.D.A., Forest Service, Intermountain Forest and Range Experiment Station. 32 pp.

3. Personal communication with Tad Weaver, October 1985.

4. D.J. Mattson and D.G. Despain. 1985. "Grizzly bear habitat component mapping handbook for the Yellowstone ecosystem." Unpublished manuscript. On file at Yellowstone National Park. 36 pp.

5. J. Weaver, R. Escano, D. Mattson, T. Puchlerz, and D. Despain. 1986. "A cumulative effects model for grizzly bear management in the Yellowstone ecosystem," pp. 234–246. In G.P. Contreras and D.E. Evans, eds. *Proceedings*. Grizzly Bear Habitat Symposium. Missoula, Montana, April 30–May 2, 1985. General Technical Report INT-207. Ogden, Utah: U.S.D.A., Forest Service, Intermountain Research Station.

Appendix I
Species List

alkali cordgrass	*Spartina gracilis*
American bistort	*Polygonum bistortoides*
arnica	
heartleaf arnica	*Arnica cordifolia*
mountain arnica	*Arnica latifolia*
arrowleaf groundsel	*Senecio triangularis*
aspen	*Populus tremuloides*
aster	
aster spp.	*Aster* spp.
Engelmann aster	*Aster engelmannii*
leafy aster	*Aster foliaceus*
showy aster	*Aster conspicuus*
western mountain aster	*Aster occidentalis*
baltic rush	*Juncus balticus*
beargrass	*Xerophyllum tenax*
bentgrass	
Ross's bentgrass	*Agrostis rossiae*
winter bentgrass	*Agrostis scabra*
bitterbrush	*Purshia tridentata*
bluegrass	
bluegrass spp.	*Poa* spp.
Cusick's bluegrass	*Poa cusickii*
Kentucky bluegrass	*Poa pratensis*
Sandberg's bluegrass	*Poa sandbergii*
timberline bluegrass	*Poa rupicola*
Wheeler's bluegrass	*Poa nervosa*
bluejoint reedgrass	*Calamagrostis canadensis*
California brome	*Bromus carinatus*
Canada thistle	*Cirsium arvense*
Cascade mountain-ash	*Sorbus scopulina*

cheatgrass	*Bromus tectorum*
chokecherry	*Prunus virginiana*
cinquefoil	
diverse-leaved cinquefoil	*Potentilla diversifolia*
graceful cinquefoil	*Potentilla gracilis*
clover	*Trifolium* spp.
common horsetail	*Equisetum arvense*
common juniper	*Juniperus communis*
common rabbitbrush	*Chrysothamnus nauseosus*
corrugate-seeded spurge	*Euphorbia glyptosperma*
creeping Oregon grape	*Mahonia repens*
dandelion	*Taraxacum officinale*
Douglas-fir	*Pseudotsuga menziesii*
downy oatgrass	*Trisetum spicatum*
early blue violet	*Viola adunca*
fescue	
Idaho fescue	*Festuca idahoensis*
sheep fescue	*Festuca ovina*
fireweed	*Epilobium angustifolium*
fringed grass-of-parnassus	*Parnassia fimbriata*
giant frasera	*Frasera speciosa*
goldenrod	
goldenrod	*Solidago missouriensis*
northern goldenrod	*Solidago multiradiata*
grouse whortleberry	*Vaccinium scoparium*
hairy golden-aster	*Chrysopsis villosa*
harebell	*Campanula rotundifolia*
huckleberry	
dwarf huckleberry	*Vaccinium caespitosum*
globe huckleberry	*Vaccinium globulare*
junegrass	*Koeleria cristata*
lanceleaf stonecrop	*Sedum lanceolatum*
liverwort spp.	*Marchantia* spp.
mallow ninebark	*Physocarpus malvaceus*
meadow barley	*Hordeum brachyantherum*
mountain dandelion	*Agoseris glauca*
mountain gooseberry	*Ribes montigenum*
mountain sweetroot	*Osmorhiza chilensis*
needlegrass	
needle-and-thread	*Stipa comata*
Richardson's needlegrass	*Stipa richardsonii*
western needlegrass	*Stipa occidentalis*

Nuttall's alkali-grass	*Puccinellia nuttalliana*
one-sided wintergreen	*Pyrola secunda*
Oregon boxwood	*Pachistima myrsinites*
phlox	
Hood's phlox	*Phlox hoodii*
many-flowered phlox	*Phlox multiflora*
pine	
limber pine	*Pinus flexilis*
lodgepole pine	*Pinus contorta*
ponderosa pine	*Pinus ponderosa*
whitebark pine	*Pinus albicaulis*
pinegrass	*Calamagrostis rubescens*
poverty danthonia	*Danthonia spicata*
prairie smoke	*Geum triflorum*
prickly rose	*Rosa acicularis*
pussytoes	
meadow pussytoes	*Antennaria corymbosa*
raceme pussytoes	*Antennaria racemosa*
rosy pussytoes	*Antennaria microphylla*
Rocky Mountain helianthella	*Helianthella uniflora*
Rocky Mountain maple	*Acer glabrum*
russet buffalo berry	*Shepherdia canadensis*
sagebrush	
big sagebrush	*Artemisia tridentata*
fringed sagebrush	*Artemisia frigida*
silver sage	*Artemisia cana*
sandwort	
arctic sandwort	*Arenaria obtusiloba*
ballhead sandwort	*Arenaria congesta*
seaside arrowgrass	*Triglochin maritimum*
sedge	
black-and-white-scaled sedge	*Carex athrostachya*
elk sedge	*Carex geyeri*
inflated sedge	*Carex vesicaria*
Nebraska sedge	*Carex nebraskensis*
Raynold's sedge	*Carex raynoldsii*
Ross's sedge	*Carex rossii*
slenderbeaked sedge	*Carex athrostachya*
water sedge	*Carex aquatilis*
sheep sorrel	*Rumex acetosella*
shiny-leaf spirea	*Spiraea betulifolia*
sickletop lousewort	*Pedicularis racemosa*

silvery lupine	*Lupinus argenteus*
snowberry	
common snowberry	*Symphoricarpos albus*
mountain snowberry	*Symphoricarpos oreophilus*
Solomon's seal	
false Solomon's seal	*Smilacina racemosa*
starry Solomon's seal	*Smilacina stellata*
spearleaf fleabane	*Erigeron lonchophyllus*
spruce	
blue spruce	*Picea pungens*
Engelmann spruce	*Picea engelmannii*
squaw currant	*Ribes cereum*
sticky geranium	*Geranium viscosissimum*
strawberry	
wild strawberry	*Fragaria virginiana*
woods strawberry	*Fragaria vesca*
subalpine fir	*Abies lasiocarpa*
sulfur buckwheat	*Eriogonum umbellatum*
sweetscented bedstraw	*Galium trifidum*
thermal western witchgrass	*Panicum occidentale*
thimbleberry	*Rubus parviflorus*
timber oatgrass	*Danthonia intermedia*
timothy	
alpine timothy	*Phleum alpinum*
timothy	*Phleum pratense*
trapper's tea	*Ledum glandulosum*
tufted hairgrass	*Deschampsia cespitosa*
twinflower	*Linnaea borealis*
twisted-stalk	*Streptopus amplexifolius*
Utah honeysuckle	*Lonicera utahensis*
weedy milkvetch	*Astragalus miser*
western meadowrue	*Thalictrum occidentale*
western red baneberry	*Actea rubra*
western serviceberry	*Amelanchier alnifolia*
western stickseed	*Lappula redowskii*
wheatgrass	
bearded wheatgrass	*Agropyron caninum*
bluebunch wheatgrass	*Agropyron spicatum*
white-flowered hawkweed	*Hieracium albiflorum*

willow
  arctic willow   *Salix arctica*
  Cascade willow   *Salix cascadensis*
  snow willow   *Salix nivalis*
woodrush
  small-flowered woodrush   *Luzula parviflora*
  spiked woodrush   *Luzula spicata*
yampa   *Perideridia gairdneri*
yarrow   *Achillea millefolium*
yellow monkeyflower   *Mimulus guttatus*
yellow spike-rush   *Eleocharis flavescens*

Appendix II
Key to Habitat Types

This key is an aid to identifying the habitat types described in this book. It has been adapted from two publications that describe the plant communities that grow on the habitat types of the region and includes most of the habitat types found in Yellowstone. It is split into two parts: forested habitat types and nonforested habitat types. Each part begins with a key to the habitat type series that are included in that part; each series of habitat types begins anew with numbered sets of choices. The distinguishing characters are plant species; therefore, a familiarity with those species is essential to use this key. The list of major species is not long and it is hoped this will not be a major stumbling block for readers.

When using the key, the choice that applies is the first one that is encountered even though a subsequent choice may also apply. For example, in part 1 the first choice is whether subalpine fir is present. A "yes" leads to the subalpine fir habitat types. A "no" leads to a choice of whether spruce is present. Spruce will probably be a part of the subalpine fir habitat types, but the second lead should only be followed if the stand has spruce but no subalpine fir.

For those not familiar with the use of a key, a short explanation is included here. This key is a dichotomous, indented key. It is a series of pairs of choices. Each pair is indented the same distance and given the same number. Choosing one of a pair leads either to the name of a type or to another pair of choices. The alternatives that relate to one part of the pair are indented under that choice. For example, if subalpine fir was reproducing successfully in the stand in question, you would go to the group of subalpine fir habitat types. However, if subalpine fir was not present, you would proceed to the choices indented under the second number 1 (i.e., those preceded by the number 2) and decide whether spruce was reproducing successfully, and so on.

Part 1. Forested Habitat Types

1. Subalpine fir present and reproducing successfully (more than ten young trees per acre)   SUBALPINE FIR HABITAT TYPES
1. Subalpine fir not the indicated climax
   2. Spruce present and reproducing successfully
                    SPRUCE HABITAT TYPES
   2. Spruce not the indicated climax
      3. Douglas-fir present and reproducing successfully
                   DOUGLAS-FIR HABITAT TYPES
      3. Douglas-fir not the indicated climax
         4. Whitebark pine 5 percent or greater cover and reproducing successfully   WHITEBARK PINE HABITAT TYPES
         4. Lodgepole pine dominant and reproducing successfully
                  LODGEPOLE PINE HABITAT TYPES

SUBALPINE FIR HABITAT TYPES

1. Bluejoint reedgrass or trapper's tea 5 percent or greater cover
                  Subalpine fir/bluejoint reedgrass
1. Bluejoint reedgrass or trapper's tea less than 5 percent cover
   2. Baneberry common   Subalpine fir/baneberry
   2. Baneberry less than 1 percent cover
      3. Twinflower common   Subalpine fir/twinflower
      3. Twinflower less than 1 percent cover
         4. Beargrass 5 percent or greater cover
                  Subalpine fir/beargrass
         4. Beargrass less than 1 percent cover
           5. Globe huckleberry 5 percent or greater cover
                  Subalpine fir/globe huckleberry
           5. Globe huckleberry less than 1 percent cover
             6. Common snowberry 5 percent or greater cover
                  Subalpine fir/common snowberry
             6. Common snowberry less than 1 percent cover
7. Western meadowrue 5 percent or greater cover
                  Subalpine fir/western meadowrue
7. Western meadowrue less than 1 percent cover
   8. Creeping Oregon grape 5 percent or greater cover
                  Subalpine fir/Oregon grape
   8. Creeping Oregon grape less than 1 percent cover
9. Grouse whortleberry 5 percent or greater cover
                  Subalpine fir/grouse whortleberry

9. Grouse whortleberry less than 1 percent cover
   10. Mountain arnica 5 percent or greater cover
                               Subalpine fir/mountain arnica
   10. Mountain arnica less than 1 percent cover
      11. Pinegrass 5 percent or greater cover
                               Subalpine fir/pinegrass
      11. Pinegrass less than 1 percent cover
         12. Elk sedge 5 percent or greater cover
                               Subalpine fir/elk sedge
         12. Elk sedge less than 1 percent cover
13. Heartleaf arnica or weedy milkvetch 5 percent or greater cover or dominant, or russet buffalo berry 5 percent or greater cover
                               Subalpine fir/heartleaf arnica
13. Not as above. Ross's sedge 5 percent or greater cover or dominant
                               Subalpine fir/Ross's sedge

SPRUCE HABITAT TYPES

1. Common horsetail greater than 25 percent cover
                               Spruce/common horsetail
1. Common horsetail not greater than 25 percent cover
   2. Sweetscented bedstraw, baneberry, or twisted-stalk greater than 1 percent cover   Spruce/sweetscented bedstraw
   2. Not as above. Twinflower greater than 1 percent cover
                               Spruce/twinflower

DOUGLAS-FIR HABITAT TYPES

1. Mallow ninebark 5 percent or greater cover
                               Douglas-fir/mallow ninebark
1. Mallow ninebark less than 1 percent cover
   2. Common snowberry 5 percent or greater cover
                               Douglas-fir/common snowberry
   2. Common snowberry less than 1 percent cover
      3. Shiny-leaf spirea 5 percent or greater cover
                               Douglas-fir/shiny-leaf spirea
      3. Shiny-leaf spirea less than 1 percent cover
         4. Pinegrass 5 percent or greater cover
                               Douglas-fir/pinegrass
         4. Pinegrass less than 1 percent cover
            5. Common juniper 5 percent or greater cover
                               Douglas-fir/common juniper
1. Grasses dominated by Idaho fescue
                               Big sagebrush/Idaho fescue

     5. Common juniper less than 1 percent cover
     6. Heartleaf arnica or weedy milkvetch 5 percent or
       greater cover or the dominant forb of normally
       depauperate undergrowths
                            Douglas-fir/heartleaf arnica
     6. Heartleaf arnica or weedy milkvetch absent or scarce.
       Mountain snowberry 5 percent or greater cover
                      Douglas-fir/mountain snowberry

WHITEBARK PINE HABITAT TYPES
  1. Grouse whortleberry 5 percent or greater cover
                      Whitebark pine/grouse whortleberry
  1. Grouse whortleberry less than 1 percent cover
                      Whitebark pine/elk sedge

LODGEPOLE PINE HABITAT TYPES
  1. Elk sedge 5 percent or greater cover   Lodgepole pine/elk sedge
  1. Elk sedge less than 1 percent cover
    2. Ross's sedge 5 percent or greater cover
                      Lodgepole pine/Ross's sedge
    2. Bitterbrush 5 percent or greater cover
                      Lodgepole pine/bitterbrush

Part 2. Nonforested Habitat Types

1. Grassland or herbland aspect; shrubs, if present, are widely scattered individuals. Half shrubs, such as fringed sage, may be abundant.
  2. Idaho fescue usually 5 percent or more cover
                 IDAHO FESCUE HABITAT TYPES
  2. Idaho fescue less than 1 percent cover
    3. Bluebunch wheatgrass usually 5 percent or more cover
             Bluebunch wheatgrass/Sandberg's bluegrass
    3. Bluebunch wheatgrass absent, sedges 5 percent or more cover
      4. Tufted hairgrass 5 percent or more cover
                     Tufted hairgrass/sedges
      4. Tufted hairgrass less than 1 percent cover
        5. Sedges forming complete cover
                   Sedge bogs and marshes
        5. Vegetation obviously on thermally influenced sites
                   Thermal communities

1. Shrubby aspect
    2. Shrubs dominated by sagebrushes
        3. Silver sage 5 percent or more cover even though big sage may be more abundant   Silver sage/Idaho fescue
        3. Silver sage absent or scarce. Big sage 5 percent or more cover
                                                    BIG SAGE HABITAT TYPES
    2. Shrubs dominated by species of willows
                                                    Willow communities

IDAHO FESCUE HABITAT TYPES
1. Bluebunch wheatgrass 5 percent or more cover
                                    Idaho fescue/bluebunch wheatgrass
1. Bluebunch wheatgrass less than 1 percent cover
    2. Tufted hairgrass present; alpine timothy and downy oatgrass also often present   Idaho fescue/tufted hairgrass
    2. Tufted hairgrass, alpine timothy, and downy oatgrass absent
        3. Richardson's needlegrass 25 percent or more cover
                                    Idaho fescue/Richardson's needlegrass
        3. Richardson's needlegrass absent or scarce. Bearded wheatgrass 5 percent or more cover
                                    Idaho fescue/bearded wheatgrass

BIG SAGEBRUSH HABITAT TYPES
1. Grasses dominated by bluebunch wheatgrass
                                    Big sagebrush/bluebunch wheatgrass

Index

Absaroka Range: alpine tundra in, 84, 93, 94; climate in, 131; forested habitat types in, 47, 48, 53; minor forested habitat types in, 56, 60, 61; nonforest habitat types in, 87

Absaroka volcanics, habitat types on, 15

air temperature, factors that determine, 128–129

alpine tundra, description of, 94. *See also* habitat types, nonforested

aspen: characteristics, 94–101; clones, 95–96; effects of wildlife on, 98–99, 100–101; in Colorado, 95; in Utah, 95; juvenility, 97; production of auxins, 97; root system, 95; survival abilities, 96–97, 100

auxins, 97

basal area: definition of, 163; relationship to precipitation, 165 (Figure 38)

Basin and Range Province, 136

Basin Creek uplift, 123

Beartooth uplift, 120, 136

Bechler meadows, habitat types in, 50, 80

big sagebrush. *See* habitat types, nonforested

Bighorn Mountains, 123

blowdown: definition of, 201; succession following, 201, 203; tree reproduction in, 202

bluebunch wheatgrass. *See* habitat types, nonforested

Cascade Range, 130; evolution of, 123

cation exchange capacity, definition of, 138

Central Plateaus, habitat types in, 46, 49, 50, 53

climax community, definition of, 5

Coastal Range, 130

cold air drainage, definition of, 125

Cole's index of association, 148–149

Columbia River–Snake River plain, 130

Continental Divide, 2, 130; in Yellowstone National Park, 131; pine beetles in, 181

Cooke City, Montana, 131

cover types: classification of, 107–108; definition of, 7; description of, 108–114

–DF, 114; fire behavior in, 114

–DF0, 113; fire behavior in, 113

–DF1, 113; fire behavior in, 113